BEYOND BOUNDARIES

Beyond Boundaries

Embracing Diversity in Pastoral Education and Supervision

Edited by
Sang Taek Lee *&* Alan Galt

Foreword by Barbara Howard

WIPF *&* STOCK · Eugene, Oregon

BEYOND BOUNDARIES
Embracing Diversity in Pastoral Education and Supervision

Copyright © 2025 Wipf and Stock Publishers. All rights reserved. Except for brief quotations in critical publications or reviews, no part of this book may be reproduced in any manner without prior written permission from the publisher. Write: Permissions, Wipf and Stock Publishers, 199 W. 8th Ave., Suite 3, Eugene, OR 97401.

Wipf & Stock
An Imprint of Wipf and Stock Publishers
199 W. 8th Ave., Suite 3
Eugene, OR 97401

www.wipfandstock.com

PAPERBACK ISBN: 979-8-3852-3969-6
HARDCOVER ISBN: 979-8-3852-3970-2
EBOOK ISBN: 979-8-3852-3971-9

VERSION NUMBER 03/19/25

Scripture quotations, unless otherwise indicated, are taken from the Holy Bible, New International Version®, NIV®. Copyright © 1973, 1978, 1984, 2011 by Biblica, Inc.™ Used by permission of Zondervan. All rights reserved worldwide. www.zondervan.com. The "NIV" and "New International Version" are trademarks registered in the United States Patent and Trademark Office by Biblica, Inc.™

Scripture quotations marked NRSV are from the New Revised Standard Version Bible, copyright © 1989 National Council of the Churches of Christ in the United States of America. Used by permission. All rights reserved worldwide.

Scripture quotations marked RSVCE are from The Catholic Edition of the Revised Standard Version of the Bible, copyright © 1965, 1966 National Council of the Churches of Christ in the United States of America. Used by permission. All rights reserved worldwide.

Scripture quotations marked KJV are from The Authorized (King James) Version. Rights in the Authorized Version in the United Kingdom are vested in the Crown. Reproduced by permission of the Crown's patentee, Cambridge University Press.

Contents

Foreword by Barbara Howard | *vii*

Acknowledgments | *ix*

List of Abbreviations | *xi*

Introduction | *xiii*

1   An Exploration of How Theological Worldviews Can Inform Clinical Pastoral Education Supervision with Special Reference to Korean Minjung Theology | 1
SANG TAEK LEE

2   Responding to *Ultimate Concerns* in Different Faiths and Cultures | 24
ALAN GALT

3   The Practice of Multifaith Spiritual Care | 36
NICOLA LE COUTEUR

4   Reflective Spaces, Liberating Spaces: How the Three Doors of Liberation Teaching Provides a Framework for Buddhist Supervisors to Deepen Their Reflective Work with Students | 50
DEBRA KELLY

5	Academic Excellence and Diversity in CPE Supervision | 65 PETER POWELL

6	Examining the Supervisee's Journey: A Hexagonal Model for Islamic Pastoral Care in CPE Supervision | 76 SALIH YUCEL

7	Diversity in Clinical Pastoral Education: A Uniting Force | 90 KRSNANGI MULDER

8	Embracing Gender Diversity in the CPE Group Context | 103 BARBARA HALL

9	A Minestrone of Mental Health Ministry | 114 ROSEMARIE SAY

10	Reflective Believing: A New Name, Not a New Method | 128 SUSANNE SCHMIDT

11	Vulnerability in Cross-Cultural Supervision | 140 MARY PEARSON

Notes on the Contributors \| 151

Foreword

When I was approached to write the foreword to this volume of essays I was drawn to the word *embracing* in the title. Here is an invitation not merely to *engage* with diversity but more significantly to *welcome and receive with open arms*1 the many and varied expressions of diversity enriching contemporary Australian society. The writers of these essays have discovered the expansion of self and community that can result from welcoming and embracing those who are "other." In a world repeatedly threatened by conflicts arising from fear of the different "other," there is an urgency in learning to *embrace* rather than repel.

As we have learned from René Girard, the other all too readily becomes a rival and then a threat to be eliminated.2 By contrast, Emmanuel Levinas reminds us of the ethical challenge constituted by the "face" of the other. He argues that it is only as we see the other as *other* than ourselves that we may truly embrace rather than "kill" the other.3 As pastoral theologian and psychologist Carrie Doehring has written,

> Levinas's use of the ethical imperative "Thou shalt not kill" continually reminds spiritual care professionals

---

1. *Oxford English Dictionary*. 2nd ed. 20 vols. Oxford: Oxford University Press, 1989, "embrace." Continually updated at http://www.oed.com/.

2. René Girard, "Mimesis and Violence," in *The Girard Reader*, ed. James G. Williams (New York: Herder and Herder, 1996), 9–19.

3. Emmanuel Levinas, *Entre Nous: On Thinking-of-the-Other*, trans. Michael B. Smith and Barbara Harshav, European Perspectives (New York: Columbia University Press, 1998), 108.

that failure to value difference can and has been part of insidious and horrifically overt webs of violence that desecrate that which is holy: the "other" that spiritual care professionals encounter.4

More recently Peter Casarella and Mun'im Sirry have urged us to "find beauty in the other"5 by opening us to the beauty to be found in diverse religious traditions.

Something of that beauty has been glimpsed by the Clinical Pastoral Education supervisors as they engage with diversity in its many expressions: cultural, social, religious, gendered, and educational. In sharing their reflections, they invite us to join with them in discovering the similarities that lie beyond the boundaries of difference. More importantly, however, they challenge us to reflect on the beauty and truth to be found in those who are different from ourselves. Such difference challenges our certainties, forces us to scrutinize our assumptions, and opens us up to hitherto unforeseen perspectives. We are enlarged by difference when we are willing to go beyond the boundaries that hem us in and dare the embrace the other.

Barbara Howard
Academic Dean
NSW College of Clinical Pastoral Education

---

4. Carrie Doehring, "The Practice of Relational-Ethical Pastoral Care," in *The Art of Spiritual Care Across Religious Difference*, rev. ed., ed. Jill L. Snodgrass (Minneapolis: Fortress, 2024), 55–81.

5. Peter Casarella and Mun'im Sirry, eds., *Finding Beauty in the Other: Theological Reflections Across Religious Traditions* (New York: Herder and Herder, 2019).

Acknowledgments

This book, titled *Beyond Boundaries: Embracing Diversity in Pastoral Education and Supervision*, was conceived and named with the aim of exploring the evolving landscape of Clinical Pastoral Education (CPE) and supervision. We are deeply grateful to the contributors who generously provided their invaluable writings. Their contributions address how CPE should respond to the diverse and changing contexts of the modern world, and we are confident that these insights will prove immensely beneficial to our readers.

We would like to take a moment to remember our dear colleague Jenny Washington who was with us when we published the first volume but has since passed away. Her absence as we bring this volume to completion is deeply felt, and we are reminded of the impact she had on all of us.

My sincere thanks go to Wipf and Stock Publishers for their enthusiastic support in bringing this second volume to fruition. We are grateful for their cooperation, which has not only allowed this work to be published but also provided an opportunity for CPE in Australia to deepen its theoretical foundations and engage in meaningful dialogue with CPE programs in other countries. Their partnership has been instrumental in fostering these important connections.

We also especially thank Barbara Howard for graciously writing the foreword and April MacNeill, Gwen Vale, and Robert MacFarlane for their endorsements on the back cover.

Finally, we wish to express our appreciation to all of our colleagues and members of the Mental Health CPE Centre for their

ACKNOWLEDGMENTS

encouragement throughout this process. We hope this book will serve as a valuable resource for supervisors as they guide their students. With heartfelt thanks, we acknowledge everyone who worked behind the scenes to make this publication possible.

Sang Taek Lee
Alan Galt
January 2025

List of Abbreviations

ACT—Australian Capital Territory

ANZACPE—Australia and New Zealand Association for Clinical Pastoral Education

CLEAR—Contract, Listen, Explore, Action, Review

CPE—Clinical pastoral education

LGBTQIA+—Lesbian, gay, bisexual, transgender, queer, intersex, asexual, and other sexually or gender diverse people

NSW—New South Wales

NSWCCPE—NSW College of Clinical Pastoral Education

PER—Pastoral encounter report

RB—Reflective believing

SA—South Australia

SBNR—Spiritual but not religious

SCD—Sydney College of Divinity

SR—Spiritual reflection

TR—Theological reflection

UN—United Nations

Introduction

In Clinical Pastoral Education, "boundaries" are the limits beyond which supervisors and pastors do not go, in order to preserve the integrity of the professional interaction. It can also refer to the ways professionals are protected from inappropriate and intrusive requests of their clients. In this book however, we are looking at the ways CPE does go beyond the traditional expectations of the role of pastoral ministry, in the past seen as the interaction of the (Christian) church with its "client" population, the now small percentage of the community who claim a commitment to a religious community.[1] The chapter authors describe various ways they are contributing to an interaction with a much wider group of Australians who indicate a need for pastoral care in a variety of crisis situations.

1. *An Exploration of How Theological Worldviews Can Inform Clinical Pastoral Education Supervision with Special Reference to Korean Minjung Theology.* Sang Taek Lee describes how the emphasis on the liberation of the oppressed in Korean Minjung theology relates to the CPE supervisors' emphasizing social justice, dignity, and the liberation of marginalized people. He looks at how CPE supervisors can respond effectively to work with the deep, unresolved grief and collective pain stemming from prolonged oppression and injustice, urging pastors to move beyond traditional

---

1. According to the 2021 Australian Census, people identified as belonging to the following: Christianity, 43.9 percent; no religion, 38.9 percent; Islam, 3.2 percent; Hinduism, 2.7 percent; and Buddhism, 2.4 percent.

views that attribute mental health issues solely to spiritual causes to a more inclusive understanding of suffering.

2. Responding to Ultimate Concerns in Different Faiths and Cultures. **Alan Galt** compares the responses of students and teachers from several faith traditions and cultures to the question, "What is the ultimate concern here—the matter beyond which nothing is more important for the person being offered pastoral ministry?" In our Mental Health CPE Centre programs, we see a remarkable similarity in the needs expressed by people from a diversity of religious and social backgrounds, as well as recognize the variety of pastoral responses available to address those needs.

3. The Practice of Multifaith Spiritual Care. Here **Nicola Le Couteur** examines what is involved in multifaith spiritual care and multifaith supervision. Multifaith engagement is based on respect for religious differences, shared moral values, and common goals, and with explicit responsibilities, ensuring spiritual care practitioners are spiritually, professionally, and ethically competent in today's diverse society.

4. Reflective Spaces, Liberating Spaces: How the Three Doors of Liberation Teaching Provides a Framework for Buddhist Supervisors to Deepen Their Reflective Work with Students. **Debra Kelly** looks at the Buddhist teaching known as the "Three Doors of Liberation," offering an Eastern perspective on what happens in the reflective supervisory space while complementing current literature. She shows how the liberating benefits of the Buddhist teaching relates to CPE supervision, for student and supervisor, via authentic connection and mutual transformation.

5. Academic Excellence and Diversity in CPE Supervision. **Peter Powell** highlights the discrepancy between our academic programs, with their Western emphasis on literary competence, and our goal based on Anton Boisen's concept of "learning from the living human documents." The emphasis on action-reflection

INTRODUCTION

methodology raises questions about the dominant Western, privileged culture surrounding CPE and challenges CPE educators to look at including people from nonliterary and colonized cultures.

6. *Examining the Supervisee's Journey: A Hexagonal Model for Islamic Pastoral Care in CPE Supervision.* **Salih Yucel** has created a service-oriented hexagonal model with the objective of comprehensively understanding the interlocutor and enhancing the pastoral care skills of both the supervisor and supervisee. He explores this hexagonal model's practical application within the context of Islamic teachings, offering insights into delivering spiritual and emotional care in CPE.

7. *Diversity in Clinical Pastoral Education: A Uniting Force.* **Krsnangi Mulder** says generosity of spirit is much needed in this, at times, turbulent world. She invites us to open our vision to the different lenses of understanding that can enhance our capacity to be love and compassion in action—to journey with quivering hearts and meet a benevolent, uniting force.

8. **Barbara Hall's** chapter, *Embracing Gender Diversity in the CPE Group Context,* describes the experience of being a pastoral educator with a student in a CPE group who identified as non-binary, a member of the LGBTQIA+ community, and a committed Christian. She notes the differences in social and professional contexts and faith group expectations between the supervisor and student and explores the ethical considerations arising.

9. *A Minestrone of Mental Health Ministry.* **Rosemarie Say** outlines her journey from being a junior psychiatric nurse to a senior mental health chaplain. She describes how forty years later her mission is to dispel stigma and to share the unique rewards of mental health ministry with students and others involved in the mental health team.

INTRODUCTION

10. In ***Reflective Believing: A New Name, Not a New Method***, **Susanne Schmidt** responds to new spiritualities and ways of reflecting. She looks at how the reflective process of CPE, traditionally called theological reflection, can move to a slight nuancing of practice that captures the zeitgeist of modern students entering into the CPE process.

11. **Mary Pearson** in ***Vulnerability in Cross-Cultural Supervision*** recognizes that gaps in understanding between people of different cultures create uncertainty and suggests that in supervision there may be assumed vulnerability for the supervisee because of perceived power imbalance. However, she also notes that there is as much vulnerability for supervisors who need to be aware of their own subconscious attitudes.

As we move beyond traditional church-based ministry to address the spiritual needs of today's diverse populations, we hope that these chapters will do more than encourage mere tolerance of differences, but also inspire and instill confidence in embracing and carrying forward the life-giving aspects of diverse traditions within newly evolving human communities.

Reverend Alan Galt
Clinical Pastoral Education Consultant

1

An Exploration of How Theological Worldviews Can Inform Clinical Pastoral Education Supervision with Special Reference to Korean Minjung Theology

SANG TAEK LEE

INTRODUCTION

This chapter explores the relationship between theological and spiritual worldviews and the practice of clinical pastoral education supervision through the lens of Korean Minjung theology. Minjung theology, a contextual theology that emerged in South Korea in the 1970s, centers on the lived experiences of the oppressed or minjung (literally, *the people*) and advocates for social justice, dignity, and the liberation of marginalized people.

Drawing on specific supervisory experiences, it examines how theology, spirituality, and philosophy influence, enlighten, and challenge the identity of a supervisor. By analyzing these influences, the chapter demonstrates how these beliefs can shape the approach to supervision. Additionally, it highlights how integrating Minjung theology with CPE provides valuable insights into the effective application of theological and spiritual worldviews.

CPE embraces vulnerable people and cares for them with God's love and compassion, which is revealed through the suffering and resurrection of Jesus Christ in the world. Anton Boisen (1876–1965), the founder of clinical pastoral education, called this concept "learning from the living human document."[1]

Boisen "wanted them [students] to learn to read human documents as well as books, particularly those revealing documents which are opened up at the inner day of judgment [of the patient]. The students were allowed to have information in regard to the case."[2] He said that "we must not begin with traditions and not with systems formulated in books, but with the open-minded exploration of living human experience in order from that to build up a body of generalizations."[3] Boisen claimed that "I have sought to begin not with the ready-made formulations contained in books but with the living human documents and with actual social conditions in all their complexity."[4]

In *The Living Human Document*, Charles Gerkin summarizes Anton Boisen's ideas into four key points: promoting open-minded discussion, avoiding rigid categorization, valuing the patient's experience on its own terms, and treating it with the same reverence as sacred texts in the Judeo-Christian tradition. For Gerkin, the marginalized are the patients in a hospital setting, focusing on the lived experiences of the vulnerable.[5]

Boisen's approach to theological reflection is not about developing doctrine or tradition, but about engaging with those in suffering and acting as their servant. Theology, therefore, should serve people in their specific contexts, offering liberation from institutional and ideological constraints. This reflection connects human struggles to divine meaning by drawing on diverse fields,

---

1. Boisen, *Exploration of the Inner World*, 10.
2. Boisen, *Exploration of the Inner World*, 10.
3. Boisen, *Exploration of the Inner World*, 251.
4. Boisen, *Exploration of the Inner World*, 185.
5. Gerkin, *Living Human Document*, 38. See also Lee and Galt, *You Visited Me*, 107.

including social sciences, psychotherapy, medicine, and the arts, to better understand and serve those on the margins.[6]

Further discussion within the context of CPE will examine how Minjung theologians, in developing Minjung theology, begin with the perspective of Jesus' ministry as portrayed in the Gospel of Mark. This perspective highlights Jesus' engagement with the socially marginalized people of his time and explores how this relates to the social and cultural characteristics of supervisees in the development of their supervisory identity. The discussion will also incorporate Korean Minjung theology as a significant theological worldview, investigating how its emphasis on the experiences of the oppressed informs and enriches pastoral care practices in the CPE setting.

1. KOREAN MINJUNG THEOLOGICAL PERSPECTIVES ON UNDERSTANDING OF *OCHLOS* AND *HAN*

In his article "Jesus and the Minjung in the Gospel of Mark," Minjung theologian Dr. Ahn Byung Mu draws a parallel between the *ochlos* (people) in the Gospel of Mark and the minjung (the oppressed people).[7] *Ochlos* is used by Mark to denote a social historical class as opposed to *laos*, which refers to a national religious group. The *ochlos*, "the minjung," are "the sinners, the tax collectors, the sick, those who opposed the powers in Jerusalem, the despised people of Galilee."[8] In Jesus' time, his ministry was exercised among the sick, the outcasts, and demon possessed (Mark 1:32–34, 5:7–13, 6:7–13). He was the friend of sinners. Jesus said to them, "It is not the healthy who need a doctor, but the sick. I have not come to call the righteous, but sinners" (Mark 2:17).

The unaccepted people such as tax collectors, sinners, women, lepers, and the unclean people had dreams and hopes of

---

6. Graham et al., *Theological Reflection*, 5–6.
7. Ahn, "Jesus and the Minjung," 136–51.
8. Ahn, "Jesus and the Minjung," 136–51.

becoming part of society, of being accepted, and having the same rights as all other people. They waited for the Messiah who would give them these opportunities in Jesus' time. In Mark's Gospel, Jesus welcomed them to be part of the kingdom of God. Minjung theologians have concluded that the minjung are those who face "socio-cultural alienation, economic exploitation, and political suppression."[9]

Minjung theology is based on the biblical references to Jesus and the *ochlos* together with the sociopolitical situation of the oppressed people of Korea. Equality is an important dimension of Minjung theology which involves just social structures and the removal of oppressive class divisions as seen in Jesus' dealings with the *ochlos*.[10]

To explain *ochlos* and *han*, Professor Suh Nam Dong explained the biblical concept of *ochlos* in the context of Korea using the concept of *han*, which reflects the suffering of the Korean people. He developed the important concept of *han* from the oppressed people (i.e., the minjung) in the Korean context.[11] *Han* "denotes the feeling of suffering of a person who has been repressed."[12] It described what is at the heart of the minjung because of their experiences. The feeling of *han* is not just an individual feeling of repression. This is not just a sickness that can be cured by psychotherapy.[13] This is a collective feeling of the oppressed in Korean society.[14]

This *han* originates from the earliest times of the Yi dynasty and is persistently intergenerational in nature. As Suh states, "This sickness of *han* can be cured only when the total structure of the oppressed society and culture is changed. . . . The feeling of *han* is an awareness both at an individual psychological level as well as at a social and political level."[15] *Han* contains several elements,

9. Suh, "Asian Theological Consultation," 39.
10. Ahn, "Jesus and the Minjung," 138–39.
11. Suh, "Asian Theological Consultation," 27.
12. Suh, "Asian Theological Consultation," 27.
13. Suh, "Asian Theological Consultation," 27.
14. Suh, "Asian Theological Consultation," 28.
15. Suh, "Asian Theological Consultation," 28.

helplessness, anger, frustration, and resignation, and contains much power which can be released, potentially for good or ill. Suh believed that "*Han* is the central experience of the Korean people as a result of centuries of foreign oppression, tyrannical rulers, discrimination against the lower classes and women, and slavery."[16] Minjung theologians regarded Jesus as the one who could bring social transformation.

Kim Yong Bock developed Suh's concept of *han* further by relating the experience of *han* to Korea's historical, social, and political contexts.[17] He provides a more concrete explanation of *han* and offers a theoretical framework. According to Kim, *han* is not merely an individual emotional state but a collective pain rooted in historical experiences and social structures. He emphasizes that *han* is a state of collective suffering resulting from social oppression and inequality. His theory emphasizes that understanding *han* requires considering both historical and structural factors. Kim, who considers the use of power and politics in relation to the minjung, distinguishes between messianic politics and political messianism in his work "Messiah and Minjung," offering insights into how political engagement and the quest for liberation intersect.[18]

Historical experiences such as colonial rule and wartime trauma in Korea can be understood through the concept of *han*. These experiences highlight how social suffering and despair transcend individual emotions to become collective and structural issues. Minjung theology interprets *han* not merely as personal anguish but as a problem intricately linked to social structures. Therefore, healing *han* requires not only personal transformation but also societal change. Integrating Minjung theology reveals that addressing *han* involves more than alleviating individual pain; it necessitates a process of structural transformation within society.

---

16. Lee, *Religion and Social Formation*, 57.
17. Kim, "Messiah and Minjung," 185–96.
18. Kim, "Messiah and Minjung," 185–96.

2. APPLICATION OF MINJUNG THEOLOGY IN CLINICAL PASTORAL EDUCATION

The perspective of Minjung theology can offer valuable insights into CPE. Minjung theology focuses on understanding the oppressed and marginalized people in Korean society, exploring their suffering and the concept of *han*. Han represents deep, unresolved grief and collective pain stemming from prolonged oppression and injustice. This perspective can be beneficial in CPE in several ways.

Minjung theology offers a broader perspective that moves beyond traditional views interpreting mental health issues merely as spiritual afflictions. It frames these issues as reflections of broader social and political oppression. In CPE, this perspective helps supervisees overcome the limitations of traditional viewpoints, encouraging a more inclusive and empathetic approach to understanding and addressing mental health concerns.

Building relationships with empathy and respect for patients is central to Minjung theology where Jesus' healing is understood not just as physical or mental restoration but as an effort to reintegrate suffering individuals into the community and restore their dignity. This understanding supports supervisees in connecting with patients through empathy and respect, rather than merely focusing on problem-solving. It guides supervisees to recognize patients' suffering as part of broader social issues and to work toward restoring their dignity.

Minjung theology emphasizes understanding in a social context, specifically understanding *han* within its social and political dimensions. This approach aids supervisees in recognizing that a patient's personal suffering is often connected to broader social issues. Supervisees learn to view patients' pain not just as individual problems but as challenges influenced by their social environment.

Reflection through Minjung theology emphasizes supporting patients' reintegration into the community and encourages supervisees to approach patients with a sense of moral responsibility. By listening to patients' experiences and acknowledging their suffering, supervisees can help restore their dignity and work to overcome social exclusion. This approach aligns with the core CPE principles of empathetic support and the role of healing.

Reflection-in-action provides a practical tool to facilitate the integration of Minjung theology perspectives into CPE, which enables a chaplain or pastoral practitioner to reflect on their pastoral encounters as they happen in real time, allowing them to be more present, empathic, and effective in their roles. Based on David Kolb's experiential learning cycle,[19] and utilized by the Australia and New Zealand Association for Clinical Pastoral Education (ANZACPE),[20] this framework is designed to help individuals navigate complex or uncertain situations by engaging in continuous reflection during practice. When applied to CPE, this approach cultivates a deeper understanding of the dynamics at play in pastoral care, particularly Minjung theology's emphasis on understanding the suffering of marginalized individuals and engaging with their *han* in a way that is compassionate and restorative.

Consequently, this represents in CPE a form of critical thinking that focuses on human values, moving beyond rigid rules and doctrines. As discussed in the previous section, in the Gospels, Jesus challenged the authoritarian and bureaucratic attitudes of the Pharisees, advocating for a more human-centered approach. Thus, CPE supervisors, unlike the Pharisees who rigidly adhered to legalism, practice a continual interpretation of human values through reflection-in-action, seeking to restore lost humanity. This foundational spirit promotes healing in wounded and divided individuals and communities, moving beyond dogmatic disputes and authoritarian or bureaucratic mindsets.

This reflective practice mirrors how Jesus connected and engaged with people, addressing their pain and the deep emotional suffering, or *han*, they experienced. His compassionate engagement serves as a model for the CPE method, which emphasizes empathy and support for those in distress, fostering a ministry that is both compassionate and human-focused. Robert Leas, in his study of Anton Boisen, referred to this as "narrative theology," and it aligns

---

19. Merriam and Bierema, *Adult Learning*, 123.
20. *ANZACPE Standards*, para. 1.

with the discipline of theological hermeneutics, which provides a language by which we connect the inner world of the other person to the outer world of experience and life events.[21] The story of *han*, the story of the minjung, the story of hurt and trauma—Minjung theology is rooted in these narratives of the people.

As we will see in the following conversation, embracing Minjung theology enables supervisees to create a more just and supportive clinical environment, addressing patients' broader experiences.

3. A CONVERSATION ON UNDERSTANDING MENTAL ILLNESS AND CPE PERSPECTIVES WITH *OCHLOS* IN MINJUNG THEOLOGY

This conversation illustrates how, while the supervisee was practicing in a mental health hospital, their initial traditional views on mental health evolved over time and how Minjung theological reflection proved helpful. The story presented here has been restructured.

> S1: In my recent clinical practice in the mental health ward, I encountered a patient who believed that someone performed witchcraft on her, leading to her delusions. Previously, I might have understood such mental health issues as manifestations of Satan's influence, a view I learned from traditional teachings. But now, I'm beginning to see things differently.
>
> L1: It's good to hear that you are reassessing your understanding. Could you tell me more about what's changing in your perspective?
>
> S2: I've realized that viewing mental illness solely through the lens of spiritual or demonic influence might be limiting. This patient's belief in witchcraft reminded me of how traditional views might have shaped my own understanding. I now see the need to understand mental

---

21. Leas, *Anton Boisen: His Life*, 191–92.

health issues in a broader context, including social and personal dimensions.

L2: It sounds like you're recognizing the limitations of a purely spiritual approach. From a Minjung theology perspective, how do you think this new understanding aligns with our practice?

S3: Minjung theology emphasizes the suffering and marginalization experienced by people. It suggests that mental health issues are not just spiritual manifestations but also reflect deeper, systemic issues. This perspective helps me see the patient's suffering as part of a larger social and historical context, not just as a spiritual problem.

L3: Exactly. Minjung theology helps us understand that suffering can be both personal and collective. It encourages us to view patients as individuals dealing with deep-rooted pain and oppression, not just as people under spiritual distress. How might this perspective influence your approach to patient care?

S4: By incorporating this understanding, I can approach patients with more empathy and respect. I'll consider their experiences within their social and personal realities rather than just attributing their issues to spiritual causes. I know that this fits with the CPE goal of providing compassionate care and supporting patients' dignity.

L4: That's a valuable shift in perspective. Minjung theology's emphasis on solidarity and transformation can guide you in addressing both individual and systemic aspects of suffering. How do you plan to integrate these insights into your practice?

S5: I plan to focus on understanding each patient's story within its broader social and historical context. I'll aim to support their emotional and psychological needs while also being mindful of the systemic issues contributing to their suffering.

L5: An excellent approach. Applying these insights will help you create a more inclusive and compassionate clinical environment. Remember, this perspective can enhance your effectiveness in providing care and support, and you are welcome to discuss any challenges you encounter as you integrate these ideas.

S6: Thank you for guiding me through this. I'll strive to apply these principles in my practice.

L6: You're welcome. I'm confident that this approach will enrich your clinical work and support meaningful transformation. Keep up the good work.

Reflection: Mental Illness and a Minjung Theological Perspective

The UN *Annual Report on Global Human Rights* (2023) underscores that mental health is a fundamental aspect of the right to health, advocating for mental health policies that protect human rights, prohibit discrimination, and preserve the dignity of individuals with mental health conditions. It also emphasizes that all individuals, regardless of their mental health status, have the right to live free from discrimination, with states required to ensure equality before the law and equal protection under the law for those with mental health conditions.[22]

The UN's emphasis on mental health as a human right, free from discrimination, and with a focus on dignity and equality, closely aligns with the core principles of Minjung theology. Minjung theology is fundamentally concerned with the dignity, liberation, and justice of marginalized and oppressed people, advocating for their full inclusion in society. Minjung theology critiques social structures that marginalize and oppress and argues for justice that brings equality and wholeness. In mental health, this means challenging stigmas and ensuring equal treatment and opportunities for those affected. Minjung theology sees healing as restoring individuals to their community, reaffirming their value and belonging.

---

22. The World Health Organization and the United Nations (UN) edited and have been actively involved in addressing mental health, human rights, nondiscrimination, and equality through various documents and reports in 2023. See chapter 2 of the report for an overview of human rights, nondiscrimination, and equality in the context of mental health.

This shared goal of reintegration promotes empathy and a more inclusive society where everyone can thrive.

Jesus often challenged the social norms and injustices of his time. He criticized systems that oppressed and excluded, advocating for the inclusion of the poor, the sick, and the outcast. This reflects Minjung theology's critique of societal structures that marginalize and the UN's call for nondiscrimination and equality. Healing the Gerasene demoniac (Mark 5:1–20) provides significant insights into Jesus' approach to healing, inclusion, and dignity. Jesus heals a man possessed by a legion of demons, living among the tombs.[23] The man, once marginalized and bound by chains, is restored to his right mind and becomes a witness to Jesus' power.

In apocalyptic literature, one of the core themes is the concept of salvation and liberation for those who are oppressed and suffering. The accounts of Jesus healing individuals possessed by demons vividly illustrate this theme of liberation.[24] Continuing with the story of the Gerasene demoniac tormented by a legion of demons, this man, living among tombs, inflicted harm upon himself and existed in profound isolation. However, Jesus' intervention restored him to his community, exemplifying a deep act of liberation.

According to apocalyptic tradition, the arrival of the kingdom of God signifies the retreat of evil forces and the beginning of a new era under divine rule. Jesus' exorcisms are closely tied to this apocalyptic vision. By casting out demons, Jesus demonstrates that the kingdom of God has already commenced through his ministry. His actions represent a part of God's plan to challenge worldly powers, defeat evil, and deliver those who are oppressed. From an apocalyptic viewpoint, Jesus' acts of healing can be interpreted as the fulfillment of the vision of salvation for the oppressed. By reaching out to those ignored and oppressed by societal powers,

---

23. Lee and Galt, *You Visited Me*, 116–20. Jesus proclaimed the new kingdom already, ruled by the Messiah, who is Jesus. The old-world order controlled by Satan has gone. Thus, the story of exorcism adopts stories of Jewish apocalyptic imagination to express the message that the kingdom has already come with Jesus, and that the old-world order has gone.

24. Lee and Galt, *You Visited Me*, 116–20.

Jesus showcases God's love and mercy. This reflects the anticipated new heaven and new earth promised by God.

In the context of Minjung theology, Jesus' actions extend beyond miraculous healing; they manifest God's concrete solidarity with the marginalized. This theological perspective frames Jesus' ministry as a process of achieving justice within the kingdom of God through solidarity with the oppressed. The man's healing reflects the UN's aim on protecting the dignity of individuals with mental health conditions and Minjung theology's emphasis on addressing and overcoming social exclusion.

Incorporating Minjung theology into CPE involves understanding mental health disorders through the lens of systemic injustice and social marginalization. Supervisors can apply this perspective by recognizing that mental health issues are often linked to broader social inequalities, fostering empathy and dignity for supervisees, and advocating for structural changes. Emphasizing cultural sensitivity and inclusion, supervisors can support supervisees by addressing their unique needs and empowering them to advocate for their own mental health. Additionally, creating a calm environment with empathy, respect, trust, and positive reinforcement corresponds with the principles of justice and compassion central to Minjung theology.

4. *HAN* AND TRAUMA: EXPLORING KOREAN SOCIETY'S PAIN AND MEMORY

Han Kang, a South Korean author who won the 2024 Nobel Prize in Literature, is known for her intense and poetic prose that confronts historical trauma and the fragility of human existence.[25] Her most celebrated works, *The Vegetarian*, *Human Acts* (originally *The Boy is Coming*), and *We Do Not Part*, delve deeply into personal and collective suffering. *Human Acts*, in particular, explores the traumatic events of the 1980 Gwangju Uprising, where students and civilians were massacred. This novel, notable for its raw

---

25. Nobel Prize Outreach AB, "Nobel Prize in Literature 2024."

depiction of violence, loss, and survival, has been praised for its profound engagement with history and memory.

As stated earlier, the concept of *han*, a traditional Korean emotion, is essential to understanding Han Kang's portrayal of trauma.[26] *Han* is defined as a deep, unresolved emotion of sorrow, resentment, anger, and pain. It arises from long-standing oppression and suffering rooted in historical experiences such as colonization, war, and dictatorship. This emotion is closely tied to the social trauma that Han Kang addresses in her works.

Through her writing, Han Kang vividly explores the collective scars left behind by historical events, particularly the pain of the Gwangju Uprising. *Han*, while a deeply personal emotion, also connects to the collective memory of Korean society, reflecting the broader historical wounds that persist over time. In *Human Acts*, she shows how the emotional and physical trauma experienced by individuals during the uprising becomes part of the collective Korean consciousness. This ongoing connection between personal suffering and social trauma mirrors the unresolved nature of *han*. She explains historical trauma as *han* in the Korean psyche.

> Cells become cancerous, attacking life. Even if the victim dies, and the body is burned, leaving only bones behind, the substance does not disappear. . . . The radiation has not yet ended. Gwangju has been resurrected and murdered countless times. It has exploded and been rebuilt in blood.[27]

Human Acts portrays not only the immediate violence of the uprising but also the enduring impact on those left behind, illustrating how *han* continues to influence both individual lives and society as a whole. By intertwining themes of grief, injustice, and the struggle for healing, Han Kang's works emphasize the

---

26. It is important to distinguish between Han Kang, the author and recipient of the 2024 Nobel Prize in Literature, and the term *han*, which is a concept in Korean culture that encapsulates a profound emotional state marked by unresolved trauma, grief, and resentment. Readers should be mindful not to conflate the two when engaging with the text.

27. Han, *Human Acts*, 207.

significance of *han* as a symbol of unresolved pain and the lasting effects of historical trauma. Through her exploration of these themes, she bridges the personal and societal dimensions of suffering, making her works a powerful reflection on the scars left by history.

Exploring the Connection Between *Han*, Trauma, and Learning Culture in Clinical Pastoral Education

Hawkins and Shohet highlight that culture is not merely something that exists within us, but rather it resides in the milieu, or the environment in which we live.[28] The French word *milieu* refers to the broader social, cultural, or physical surroundings that shape our experiences. Hawkins suggests that supervision and learning thrive in environments that foster a culture of development and growth. In particular, a learning culture that encourages learning both individually and collectively from everyday work experiences.[29]

This idea of culture and environment is deeply connected to the themes of *han* and trauma found in Han Kang's works such as *Human Acts*. The unresolved pain and collective suffering represented by *han* are tied to the social and historical milieu of Korean society. Similarly, these concepts provide valuable insights for CPE, as they help students empathize with both individual and collective suffering on a deeper level. By understanding the historical context behind unresolved trauma, CPE practitioners can provide more meaningful care, addressing not only personal wounds but also broader societal and historical dimensions of pain.

Therefore, the milieu in which learning and pastoral care occur is essential for both individual and collective growth. Through this broader understanding of suffering, CPE supervisees can foster compassionate, effective pastoral care that encompasses both personal grief and the collective scars left by history.

---

28. Hawkins and Shohet, *Supervision*, 106.
29. Hawkins and Shohet, *Supervision*, 202.

Korean National Trauma as *Han* in Clinical Pastoral Education

This case study will examine how historical experiences can be understood through the concept of *han*, connecting these experiences to collective and structural issues. In particular, the trauma experienced by the Korean minjung (stemming from conflicts, wars, and the ongoing struggle between North and South Korea) serves as a significant example of *han* as collective suffering.

Korea was liberated from Japan on August 15, 1945, a day celebrated annually as the National Liberation Day of Korea in both North and South Korea. However, the Korean War, which began on June 25, 1950, has caused ongoing generational trauma due to the continued conflict and division between the two Koreas. This trauma, a significant part of the cultural concept of *han*, represents the negative emotional feelings held by people in both Koreas against one another. This *han* becomes nationally and socially embedded in the division between South and North Koreans.

A young Korean pastor (P), during individual supervision, shared his experience with a debate in South Korean churches about North Korea. In his June sermon, he urged churches, including those in Sydney, to help suffering North Koreans.

An elder who lost his father in the Korean War criticized the pastor, arguing that the pastor did not understand the war's tragedy, and viewed North Korea's famine as divine punishment. The elder questioned why they should offer help. The pastor raised his ministry issue with me and part of the conversation record is here as follows:

> P1: Yes, I had trouble with an elder after a sermon about supporting North Korea. He said, "Pastor, today's sermon disappointed me."
>
> L1: You feel disappointed with his response.
>
> P2: Yes, I preached about humanitarian support for North Korea. The elder believes God is judging North Korea with famine and doesn't understand my perspective.
>
> L2: What has the elder experienced in his life?

P3: He fled North Korea during the war, lost his father, grew up in hardship, joined the army, and then immigrated to Australia. He really hates North Korea.

L3: Can you reflect on the elder's life?

P4: The trauma of the Korean War affects those who lived through it, like the elder. It makes reconciliation difficult.

L4: What are the barriers to the elder's healing?

P5: Many South Koreans see North Korea as evil. This ongoing pain is our tragedy.

L5: Could you consider the elder's perspective?

P6: I engaged him in theological debates without considering his trauma. I regret my strong reaction.

Evaluation of This Conversation

In this encounter, P expressed distress over a conflict with an elder regarding his sermon advocating support for North Korea, a nation facing famine and food crises. The elder's disapproval left P feeling angry and disappointed, as he believed his preaching reflected God's compassion to help those in need, even perceived enemies like North Koreans.

However, P recognized the elder's deep-seated animosity toward North Korea, rooted in his traumatic experiences during the Korean War. Through our conversation, P realized the generational trauma still affecting both North and South Koreans. He acknowledged the barriers hindering healing including pervasive ideologies and historical grievances.

As our discussion unfolded, P came to understand the need to empathize with the elder's perspective and acknowledged his own role in exacerbating tensions through theological debates. Eventually, P expressed a desire to reconcile and apologized for his previous lack of understanding. This transformative journey demonstrates the healing potential of compassionate communication and the ethos of CPE paving the way for reconciliation and mutual understanding.

5. UTILIZING THE CLEAR SUPERVISION MODEL TO EXPLORE THE ELDER'S *HAN*: DISAPPOINTMENT, ANXIETY, AND ANGER

Minjung theologians have identified the concept of *han* from the lived experiences of the people in the Korean context. *Han* is a concept that encompasses not only individual suffering but also extends to social dimensions. The history of Korea is marked by suffering, and the conflict and war between the North and South have created a deep *han* in the hearts of the people.

Minjung theology identifies *han* as the ultimate concern of the minjung—the oppressed and marginalized people in Korean society. *Han* embodies a profound, unresolved grief and bitterness stemming from prolonged oppression and injustice. It is both a personal and collective experience reflecting the suffering of the minjung who have faced social, political, and economic hardships throughout Korea's history. By addressing *han* as their ultimate concern, Minjung theology aims to facilitate healing, liberation, and justice in line with its broader commitment to solidarity and transformation in the lives of the oppressed.

The aim of CPE is not to resolve human emotions through psychological analysis. While utilizing psychological and counseling methodologies, it operates within a different boundary and approach. Alan Galt explains that the realm of CPE involves discovering the patient's ultimate concerns through theological reflection and to foster spiritual strength within the patient. He states that the focus on the person's "ultimate concern" is a way of understanding what the person really needs from effective pastoral care, recognizing that "ultimate concerns" vary with peoples' life situation, and that a patient or resident may be at a very different stage of their life than the person offering pastoral care.[30] In CPE, spiritual strength is considered as the process of

---

30. Lee and Galt, *Beyond Boundaries*, 28. The term *ultimate concern* was coined by Paul Tillich in his book *Theology of Culture*, 6–7, and Galt has adopted Tillich's term as his template. Tillich made this statement in his address at the National Conference on Clinical Pastoral Education, Atlantic City, New Jersey, in November 1956.

listening, accompanying, and empathizing, allowing the person to resolve their encountered events themselves. We refer to this kind of spiritual strengthening provided by CPE supervision as being a "ministry of presence."

Hawkins and Shohet explain the methods of CPE through the CLEAR supervision model. By applying their methods, we aim to examine how the supervisor addresses the issues brought by the supervisee. The CLEAR supervision model was employed for the encounter with P which is described above. This model consists of five stages: *Contract, Listen, Explore, Action,* and *Review*.[31]

In the *contract* stage, both the supervisee and the supervisor agreed to discuss concerns related to the supervisee's ministry. They clarified the supervisee's needs for the session, focusing on issues pertinent to his ministry.

Moving to the *listen* stage, the supervisee needed to understand the elder's perspective. During the encounter, P expressed feelings of sadness, anger, and disappointment toward the elder. While initially struggling to see the elder's perspective, P was gradually prompted to consider the elder's suffering and underlying feelings.

Transitioning to the *explore* stage, the implications of P's actions were explored, fostering awareness. As P began to consider the elder's feelings, he was encouraged to reflect on his own emotions and their impact on the elder.

In the subsequent *action* stage, P decided to apologize to the elder for not understanding him.

This decision was clarified in the *review* stage, where P confirmed his intention to contact and meet with the elder, ensuring clarity in his chosen course of action.

This application of the CLEAR supervision model facilitated P's reflection and decision-making process, leading to a resolution of the conflict with the elder. Through this structured approach, P gained valuable insights and formulated a clear plan for reconciliation and understanding within his pastoral relationships.

---

31. Hawkins and Shohet, *Supervision*, 61.

During the process, P came to understand that the elder harbored deep pain and suffering, thus leading him to empathize with the elder's traumatic experiences. Recognizing that theological debates alone could not resolve the situation, the pastor acknowledged the importance of listening to the elder's feelings and supporting him on a path to healing and understanding.

During their interaction, it became clear that P experienced emotional turmoil including disappointment, anxiety, and anger, and faced a challenge. His preaching, rooted in the Christian principle of helping one's neighbor as taught by Jesus, conflicted with the elder's differing theological views. During supervision, I helped P shift his focus to grasp the elder's perspective and thus fostered mutual emotional awareness. Looking ahead, the goal was to help P gradually reconsider his approach to engaging with the elder. Through emphasizing empathy, compassion, and building genuine connections, CPE bridges ideological divides by promoting active listening, empathy, and mutual respect.

The elder will continue to mature with the spiritual support of the faith community (through prayer, love, visits, fellowship, and Bible study). Through these spiritual resources of the church, the Holy Spirit will help the elder walk the path of maturity. The supervisee (pastor) will also grow in maturity by learning pastoral wisdom through repeated action and reflection. The relationship between P and the elder will continue to develop toward maturity within the faith community through both receiving ongoing support and care. We can call this process the supervisory process, which is the process of growing with the community.

The *han* in the context of North-South Korean relations cannot be healed solely through doctrinal theories or policy approaches. Ideological or missionary methods may even exacerbate the conflict. The CLEAR supervision model, however, has demonstrated its effectiveness in resolving conflicts, as seen in the case of the resolution between the elder and the young pastor. Thus, the approaches utilized in CPE can assist supervisors in addressing conflicts between supervisees and clients. This approach shows promise as a valuable method for addressing the social conflicts and the North-South Korean divide experienced by the Korean people.

The principles and methods in CPE supervision offer a pathway toward peace and unity, fostering genuine connections that transform divided relationships into a cohesive community. God desires to embrace the separated community with his compassion, reconciling us to himself through Christ.[32] Just as the Trinity demonstrates how to rebuild one community from separation, CPE supervision provides a framework for addressing national traumas and working toward reconciliation grounded in compassion and respect.

By embracing these principles and methods, individuals can engage in meaningful dialogue, empathy, and mutual respect, transcending ideological differences and fostering harmony. Through supervision, individuals are enabled to participate in the ministry of building a community where the Trinity is at work. Through their ministry, pastoral carers are called to establish God's kingdom on earth, partnering with the Triune God. Supervisors, working together with the Trinity as revealed in Jesus, must remember that "pastoral supervision is relational,"[33] with three interlocking dimensions: the suffering people, the pastoral worker (supervisor), and God of the Trinity (working in the human context with love).[34]

CONCLUSION

This chapter has explored the integration of theological and spiritual perspectives within clinical pastoral education supervision with a focus on Korean Minjung theology. Minjung theology introduces the concepts of *han* and *ochlos*. *Han* denotes a profound, collective, and individual suffering that transcends personal emotions and reflects universal experiences of anger, disappointment, and pain. *Ochlos* refers to the marginalized or common people,

---

32. Paul highlights this concept in 2 Cor 5:18–20.
33. Rose, "Theological Framework," 27.
34. Rose, "Theological Framework," 28.

highlighting their collective struggles and the social injustices they face. These concepts in Minjung theology together provide a framework for understanding and addressing the deep-seated issues faced by supervisees during pastoral care and raised during supervision.

By incorporating Minjung theology into CPE supervision, this chapter illustrates how focusing on *han*, which *ochlos* has felt, can provide critical insights for addressing profound grief and suffering that supervisees may encounter in patient interactions during pastoral care. It emphasizes the need to move beyond doctrinal or missional interpretations that may exacerbate conflicts, particularly in the context of ongoing tensions between North and South Korea. As discussed above, *han* in North-South Korean relations cannot be healed through doctrinal theories or policy approaches alone, as these may worsen conflicts.

By integrating Minjung theology and CPE principles, supervisors and supervisees can create a more inclusive and supportive clinical environment, and may also be useful within broader social and political contexts like the North-South Korean divide. This approach fosters a deeper understanding and solidarity with the collective and personal suffering of those in society, ultimately contributing to healing and reconciliation. Supervisors and supervisees are reminded that they are called to be advocates for reconciliation, working to build God's community in the world in our society (2 Cor 5:18–20).

BIBLIOGRAPHY

Ahn, Byung Mu. "Jesus and the Minjung in the Gospel of Mark." In *Minjung Theology: People as the Subjects of History*, edited by Yong Bock Kim, 136–51. Singapore: Christian Conference of Asia, 1981.

Australia and New Zealand Association for Clinical Pastoral Education. *ANZACPE Standards—Foundational and Advanced CPE 2022.* https://www.anzacpe.org.au/wp-content/uploads/2022/11/2022-Standards-Foundational-Advanced-CPE.pdf.

Boisen, Anton T. *The Exploration of the Inner World.* New York: Willett, Clark, 1936.

Galt, Alan. "Demystifying Mental Health Ministry." Paper for the SCD Learning and Teaching Conference, Sydney, Sept. 27–28, 2013. Revised 2018.
Gerkin, Charles V. *The Living Human Document: Re-Visioning Pastoral Counseling in a Hermeneutical Mode*. Nashville: Abingdon, 1984.
Graham, Elaine, et al. *Theological Reflection: Methods*. London: SCM, 2005.
Han, Kang. *Human Acts*. Translated by Deborah Smith. London: Portobello, 2017.
―――. *The Vegetarian*. Translated by Deborah Smith. London: Portobello, 2016.
―――. *We Do Not Part*. Translated by E. Yaewon and Paige Aniyah Morris. London: Penguin, 2025.
Hawkins, Peter, and Robin Shohet. *Supervision in the Helping Professions*. 3rd ed. Maidenhead, UK: Open University Press, 2006.
Hewson, Daphne, and Michael Carroll. *Reflective Practice in Supervision*. Hazelbrook, Australia: MoshPit, 2016.
Kee, Howard Clark. *Community of the New Age: Studies in Mark's Gospel*. Macon, GA: Mercer University Press, 1983.
Kim, Yong Bock. "Messiah and Minjung: Discerning Messianic Politics Over Against Political Messianism." In *Minjung Theology: People as the Subjects of History*, edited by Yong Bock Kim, 185–96. Singapore: Christian Conference of Asia, 1981.
Leach, Jane, and Michael Paterson. *Pastoral Supervision: A Handbook*. 2nd ed. London: SCM, 2015.
Leas, Robert David. *Anton Theophilus Boisen: His Life, Work, Impact, and Theological Legacy*. Decatur, GA: Outskirts, 2009.
Lee, Sang Taek. *Religion and Social Formation in Korea: Minjung and Millenarianism*. Religion and Society 37. Berlin: Mouton de Gruyter, 1996.
Lee, Sang Taek, and Alan Galt, eds. *You Visited Me: Encouraging Spiritual Practice in a Secular World*. Eugene, OR: Wipf and Stock, 2021.
Merriam, Sharan B., and Laura L. Bierema. *Adult Learning: Linking Theory and Practice*. Hoboken, NJ: John Wiley and Sons, 2014.
Nobel Prize Outreach AB. "The Nobel Prize in Literature 2024." Press release, Oct. 10, 2024. https://www.nobelprize.org/prizes/literature/2024/press-release.
Powell, Peter. *Story Whispering: An Introduction to Biblical-Narrative Therapy*. North Parramatta, Australia: Pastoral Counselling Institute, 2014.
Rose, Jessica. "Rooted and Grounded in Love: A Theological Framework for Pastoral Supervision." In *Enriching Ministry: Pastoral Supervision in Practice*, edited by Michael Paterson and Jessica Rose, 21–39. London: SCM, 2014.
Suh, David Kwang-sun. "A Biographical Sketch of an Asian Theological Consultation." In *Minjung Theology: People as the Subjects of History*, edited by Yong Bock Kim, 17–40. Singapore: Christian Conference of Asia, 1981.

Suh, Nam Dong. "Towards a Theology of Han." In *Minjung Theology: People as the Subjects of History*, edited by Yong Bock Kim, 51–66. Singapore: Christian Conference of Asia, 1981.

Tillich, Paul. *Theology of Culture*. London: Oxford University Press, 1964.

United Nations Office of the High Commissioner for Human Rights. *UN Human Rights Report 2023*. Geneva: United Nations Office, 2023. https://www.ohchr.org/sites/default/files/documents/publications/ohchr-reports/ohchr-report-2023.pdf.

2

Responding to *Ultimate Concerns* in Different Faiths and Cultures

ALAN GALT

INTRODUCTION

In our Mental Health CPE Centre programs, we have observed how people from diverse religious and social backgrounds have a remarkable similarity in their deepest spiritual needs, and that there is a range of pastoral responses available to address those needs. We devised a tool to help CPE supervisors, educators and consultants recognize and respond to the variety of approaches relevant to the people who need pastoral care.

1. THE CENTRALITY OF THEOLOGICAL REFLECTION IN CLINICAL PASTORAL EDUCATION

When my daughter started as an education consultant with a government accredited body that helps teachers from smaller schools to upgrade their teaching credentials, she told me excitedly, "I'm doing what you do, Dad." I proudly agreed. We are both empowering our people to meet particular education goals, hers the government requirements, and mine helping our supervisors to teach students; and our educators to develop supervisory programs.

Our core emphases differ: the state education department teaches kids, young adults, and even seniors what they need to know to survive in a secular world, whereas clinical pastoral education responds to the "spiritual dimension" of human needs, centering on "ultimate concerns," what is the most important issue for the supervisee. Our focus in dealing with the people going through health and similar crises is "what is the most significant issue for you at the moment, and what pastoral resources would be appropriate to meet your concern?" Abraham Maslow's "hierarchy of human needs"[1] recognizes that more "basic" needs have to be met before the "higher" needs can be addressed. As William Booth declared in 1860, echoing the epistle of Jas 2:16, "You cannot warm the hearts of people with God's love if they have an empty stomach and cold feet."[2] Our concentration is on the "higher" need for self-actualization, finding purpose and meaning, even in the most discouraging life circumstances[3] and includes Maslow's[4] later addition to his list: "self-transcendence—seeing ourselves as part of the broader universe to develop the common priorities that can allow humankind to survive as a species."[5]

2. LOOKING CLOSELY AT THE ULTIMATE CONCERN: WHAT IS THE MOST IMPORTANT QUESTION FOR THIS PERSON, AT THIS TIME?

This remains the most difficult aspect of a CPE unit for many students. Over a decade, our Mental Health CPE Centre has

---

1. Maslow, *Motivation*; Maslow, *Religions*.
2. Salvation Army Australia, *Annual Report*, 2.
3. Corey, *Theory and Practice*, 144 (discussing Viktor Frankl).
4. Maslow, *Human Nature*.
5. Berman, "Maslow's Hierarchy," para. 5.

developed a system enabling supervisors and educators to help pastoral visitors move on from the patients' most immediate, often most dramatic, concerns, to focus on what is really most important for them to deal with. We have devised a spiritual reflection template (table 1),[6] incorporating the input of the pastoral writers[7] as well as our own experience of what empowers and inspires the people we visit.

---

6. Mental Health CPE Centre, "Theological/Spiritual Reflection Template."
7. Jennings, "Pastoral Theological Methodology," 862–64; Graham et al., *Theological Reflection*.

Table 1: Theological/Spiritual Reflection Template

Theological/Spiritual Reflection Template: The Mental Health CPE Centre (2020)

1. The Incident, Event or Specific Interaction (arising in your pastoral visit)

Give a brief account of a significant event or situation that you have experienced in the past few weeks, as if you are describing it to someone who was not there but who would be very interested to hear what you want to say.

2. Its Impact on Me—How You Felt in That Situation

Describe its impact on you—how it affected you, what you felt about it. Use phrases like "I felt..." "I was..." plus a word or phrase describing how you felt, such as "saddened, excited, distressed, delighted, angry, overjoyed," or "confused, perplexed, numb..."

3. Ultimate Concerns Present

Significant issues beyond which nothing is more important. This will be influenced by where the person is at in life (Maslow's "Hierarchy of Needs"). This exercise also asks you, the pastoral visitor, to look at where the specific interaction fits with your own spiritual journey.

4. Spiritual Reflection

What spiritual truths apply in this situation? What message from your faith, or from the faith of the resident or others involved, is relevant?

or Theological Reflection

Where is God in this situation? What do the teaching of the Scriptures and the traditions of your faith say about such occurrences? How does your common sense and your secular understanding relate to your perception of what is God's word in this event?

5. Pastoral Resources Needed Here

For example, pastoral presence; pastoral conversation; prayer; stories and examples from the Scriptures and sacred teachings; religious ritual, liturgy, sacrament; discussion of spiritual themes.

The term *spiritual reflection* acknowledges the interest in pastoral education of Buddhists and others from a nontheistic tradition. Our focus on the person's *ultimate concern*[8] is a way of understanding what they really need from effective pastoral care. We recognize that *ultimate concerns* vary with peoples' life situations, and that a patient or resident may be at a very different stage of their life than the person offering pastoral care.

In this exercise, students present reports on their pastoral encounters using the five-point spiritual reflection template that we have developed. Table 2 is a sample of my summaries of recent reports presented in group supervision.

Table 2: Summary of Students' Theological/Spiritual Reflection Templates Reported in Group Supervision

Student, age, unit, tradition	Summary of Interaction, and Impact on Student	Ultimate Concern	Spiritual Reflection, and Pastoral Resources
May[9] 60 CPE 1 Buddhist Vietnamese counselor	Distressed Buddhist community member anxious that witches were interfering with his medical treatment. Compassion and helplessness.	Where can hope be found? Can I trust the doctors who don't take my fear seriously?	Three "poisons": greed, hatred, and ignorance, can be healed by three "wholesome attitudes": generosity, loving kindness, and wisdom.

---

8. Tillich, *Theology of Culture*, 6–7.
9. Pseudonyms are used throughout this chapter.

Julie 53 CPE 1 Chinese migrant Evangelical Protestant Christian	Self-loathing psychiatric patient talking of suicide to escape the pain in his soul. Shock, sadness, and helplessness.	*How can I get rid of this destructive guilt and self-condemnation?*	Soul peace can only come by reconnecting with our Creator. Prayer and Scripture can release from spiritual battle. Suffering can produce growth. Compassionate presence. Confession, repentance, accept forgiveness.
Mervin 74 CPE 3 Retired professional, pastoral visitor Catholic Christian layman	Moderately dementing and physically deteriorating aged care resident feels abandoned. Vulnerable and helpless to change his situation.	*Need for safety, dignity, to be validated as a person.*	The Lord's strength is the answer to our human frailty. Pastoral accompaniment, encouraging meaning, purpose, connection.
Paulos 30 CPE 1 Health professional Orthodox theological student	A moderately dementing aged care resident, with labile emotions, confusing me with her son. I felt helpless and unsure how to respond without upsetting her.	*The frailty of the human mind. How can God allow this to happen?* *The inevitability of the aging process.*	God is there, despite our "fall" from innocence, and he has sent his Son to restore us. Respectful and compassionate pastoral presence. Gentle teaching. Validating her talents. Promoting fellowship.

Jacob 55 CPE 2 Korean parish minister	Parishioner hit by another car, shaken and scared. Reminded that humans are always vulnerable.	*Continuing pain and fear of driving. Loss of confidence in herself.*	It could have been worse. Responders were soon on the spot. Optimistic prayer, laying on of hand, supportive community. Advice and information about recovering from the trauma.
Nahum 60 Introductory CPE Jewish rabbi	School girl grieving over her mother's death in a car accident. Unresolved questions about how "G‑d" could let this happen. Sad, helpless and without a satisfying answer. Hoping that her family and friends were supportive.	*How can she survive and recover and not lose faith, become depressed, fearful, and mentally paralysed?*	There is no answer. It's OK to be angry with "G‑d." The eternity of the soul. Gentle encouragement. Ritual in memory and action in honor of her mother. Speaking with the rabbi's wife.
Mohammed 50 CPE 1 Muslim imam	Friend confiding that he wanted to have no regrets on his death bed, and confessed his lack of spiritual conviction. Sad to see his state of heedlessness to the faith.	*The emptiness and purposelessness of life without God.*	This earthly life is deceptive and misleading. Brief advice on the spot. Offer ongoing conversation about life's real purpose (to do what God wants).

3. DEALING WITH THE SPIRITUAL ISSUES INVOLVED IN THIS SITUATION

Students respond succinctly and accurately to each segment, with succeeding steps building on the previous one. This produces a precise and relevant reflection on the pastoral encounter, which allows supervisees to assess the effectiveness of their pastoral response. The five steps together allow a consistent and effective progress from the incident itself to what pastoral responses could be applied.

The fifth step, "Pastoral Resources Needed," invites students to be adventurous, perhaps to devise new, appropriate ways to encourage patients to recognize and deal with their ultimate concerns, as in the recent book by Paterson and Crumlish describing imaginative methods of supervision, where Michael gives a personal illustration of the value of creative pastoral supervision for himself:

> I logged on to the session with a story of loss. I'm logging off with the realisation of something found.[10]

In the past five years I have used this five-step method of reflection on pastoral encounters with students from a range of faith traditions with surprising similarities in what is identified as the "ultimate concern," but significant differences in understanding what pastoral resources would be helpful.

4. COMPARISON OF THE USE OF THE THEOLOGICAL/SPIRITUAL REFLECTION TEMPLATE BY STUDENTS FROM DIVERSE FAITH TRADITIONS

Students from seven very different faith traditions used the spiritual reflection template to identify the ultimate concerns present and to choose pastoral resources to meet those concerns (table 3).

---

10. Paterson and Crumlish, *Pastoral Supervision*, 12.

Table 3: Comparison of Ultimate Concern Identified and Teaching of the Faith Tradition

Student's Tradition	Ultimate Concern Identified	Teaching of the Faith Tradition
Buddhist	Where can hope be found? Can I trust the doctors who don't take my fear seriously?	"Buddhist chaplains offer emotional and spiritual support, loving-kindness and compassion. They bring a caring presence and willingness to listen, especially during times of difficulty. Chaplains may be ordained monastics (monks and nuns) or lay people."[11]
Evangelical Protestant	How can I get rid of destructive guilt and self-condemnation?	Biblically and theologically informed pastoral care that alleviates distress and promotes wellbeing, especially to those suffering from mental illness.[12]
Catholic	Need for safety, dignity, to be validated as a person.	Hospital chaplaincy and pastoral care is the ministry of presence: building relationships; listening to life stories without judgment; articulating empathy and respect; nourishing, sustaining, and guiding, particularly in times of grief and trauma; engaging a Catholic priest; enlivening the spirit; and providing sacraments, ritual, and prayer when requested.[13]
Orthodox	The frailty of the human mind. How can God allow this to happen? The inevitability of the aging process.	"The purpose of pastoral care is to cultivate the healing, transforming presence of the living Christ in the lives of the people within the parish and beyond. In the Orthodox Church, the sacraments and liturgical services are central to pastoral care."[14]
Korean Protestant	Continuing pain and fear of resuming driving. Loss of confidence in herself.	*Minjung* han theology sees the liberation of the poor, oppressed, and suffering parallel to the life and work of Jesus.[15]

11. Buddhist Council of NSW, "Chaplaincy Program."

12. Anglican Deaconess Ministries, "Mental Health and Pastoral Care Institute."

13. CatholicCare Diocese of Broken Bay, "Hospital Chaplaincy."

14. Saint Sophia Hellenic Orthodox Church, "Pastoral Care."

15. Lee and Galt, *You Visited Me*, 123.

Jewish rabbi	How to survive and recover and not lose faith, become depressed, fearful, and mentally paralyzed.	"Pastoral Care is a person-centred, holistic approach to caring for clients that compliments [sic] the care offered by other helping disciplines while paying particular attention to spiritual care. The focus of pastoral care is the healing, guiding, supporting, nurturing, liberating and empowering of our elders and clients."[16]
Muslim imam	The emptiness and purposelessness of life without God.	Muslim spiritual and religious care givers assess and determine spiritual and religious needs, develop and implement suitable and appropriate spiritual care.[17]

There is a remarkable consistency in what students were feeling: helpless, sad, uncertain, vulnerable, shocked, inadequate, concerned. These were what would be expected from researchers in the field of multicultural supervision, Ladany and Bradley,[18] and Mabry.[19]

The ultimate concerns identified were also similar: the need for hope, trust, validation, dignity, confidence to survive. People visited were consistently asking the same questions. Where can hope be found? Who can I trust? How can I be rid of destructive guilt and self-condemnation? Where can I be safe, feel dignity, be validated? The frailty of the human condition, the inevitability of the aging process. How can God allow this to happen? Loss of self-confidence. How to survive and recover and not lose faith, become depressed, fearful, and mentally paralyzed. The emptiness and purposelessness of life without God.

I wonder if an independent reader would be able to identify which student has elicited which response.

16. Jewish Care, "Pastoral Care."
17. Isgandarova, "Effectiveness of Islamic Spiritual Care."
18. Ladany and Bradley, *Counselor Supervision*.
19. Mabry, *Spiritual Guidance*.

CONCLUSION

I am careful not to generalize about the results of examining the students' answers. We cannot say this is proof that people from diverse faiths see the same *ultimate concern*. There is an obvious intervening variable: all the students were in programs I supervised, so it is not surprising that they identified similar spiritual needs and relevant pastoral resources.

However, the exercise did indicate that students from diverse faith traditions can recognize and respond appropriately to the pastoral/spiritual needs of their patients or residents going through times of sickness or crisis. Their pastoral responses reflect the traditions from which they come, but there *is* a similarity between the perceptions of students from various traditions about what distresses people most in their crises, and what it entails to accompany them effectively.

Specific Conclusions for Our Clinical Pastoral Education Training

1. *By working through the five steps*, pastors are helped to home in on what their patients, residents, inmates, or parishioners want to talk about and to clarify what would be suitable responses.

2. *Using this template*, supervisors have a focus for their work with chaplains and pastoral visitors, identifying the issues that are really important for them.

3. *Pastoral educators* are using this tool in CPE programs to facilitate consistent, effective reflective practice.

BIBLIOGRAPHY

Anglican Deaconess Ministries. "The Mental Health and Pastoral Care Institute." https://mentalhealthinstitute.org.au.

Berman, Robby. "The Missing Apex of Maslow's Hierarchy Could Save Us All." Big Think, Feb. 13, 2017. https://bigthink.com/personal-growth/the-missing-apex-of-maslows-hierarchy-could-save-us-all.

Buddhist Council of NSW. "Chaplaincy Program." https://www.buddhistcouncil.org/chaplaincy-program.

CatholicCare Diocese of Broken Bay. "Hospital Chaplaincy and Pastoral Care." https://catholiccaredbb.org.au/individual-family-supports/hospital-chaplaincy-pastoral-care.

Chowdhury, Madhuleena Roy. "4 Appreciative Inquiry Tools, Exercises and Activities." Apr. 27, 2019. https://positivepsychology.com/appreciative-inquiry-tools/.

Corey, Gerald. *Theory and Practice of Counseling and Psychotherapy*. 10th ed. Boston: Cengage, 2021.

Graham, Elaine, et al. *Theological Reflection: Methods*. London: SCM, 2005.

Isgandarova, Nazila. "Effectiveness of Islamic Spiritual Care: Foundations and Practices of Muslim Care Givers." *Journal of Pastoral Care and Counseling* 66 (2012) 1–16.

Jennings, T. W. "Pastoral Theological Methodology." In *Dictionary of Pastoral Care and Counseling*, expanded ed., edited by Rodney J. Hunter, 862–64. Nashville: Abingdon, 2005.

Jewish Care. "Jewish Life: Pastoral Care." https://www.jewishcare.org.au/services/jewish-life.

Ladany, Nicholas, and Loretta J. Bradley, eds. *Counselor Supervision*. 4th ed. New York: Routledge, 2010.

Lee, Sang Taek, and Alan Galt, eds. *You Visited Me: Encouraging Spiritual Practice in a Secular World*. Eugene, OR: Wipf and Stock, 2021.

Mabry, John R., ed. *Spiritual Guidance Across Religions: A Sourcebook for Spiritual Directors and Other Professionals Providing Counsel to People of Differing Faith Traditions*. Woodstock, VT: SkyLight Paths, 2014.

Maslow, Abraham H. *The Farther Reaches of Human Nature*. New York: Viking, 1971.

———. *Motivation and Personality*. New York: Harper and Row, 1954.

———. *Religions, Values, and Peak-Experiences*. Columbus: Ohio State University Press, 1964.

Mental Health CPE Centre. "Template for Spiritual Reflection." 2020.

NSW College of Clinical Pastoral Education. "Institutional Moderation Action Plan." Unpublished working paper, NSWCCPE, 2015.

Paterson, Michael, and Liz Crumlish. *Pastoral Supervision: Creativity in Action*. Edinburgh: Institute of Pastoral Supervision and Reflective Practice, 2021.

Saint Sophia Hellenic Orthodox Church. "Pastoral Care." https://www.saintsophianl.org/copy-of-pastoral-care.

Salvation Army Australia. *Annual Report 2024*. Salvation Army Australia Communications Department, Dec. 2024. https://www.salvationarmy.org.au/scribe/sites/auesalvos/files/images/annual-report/2024-TSA_Annual_Report_VFinal_Interactive__WS.pdf.

Tillich, Paul. *Theology of Culture*. London: Oxford University Press, 1964.

Walton, Heather. *Writing Methods in Theological Reflection*. London: SCM, 2014.

3

The Practice of Multifaith Spiritual Care

NICOLA LE COUTEUR

INTRODUCTION

This chapter examines the implications for spiritual care supervision of multifaith spiritual care. As an intentional activity, multifaith engagement is based on the recognition of and respect for religious and spiritual differences, nonetheless cooperating on a foundation of shared moral values and a willingness to work toward common goals. Using examples from my supervisory practice, I demonstrate that the supervision of multifaith practitioners has responsibilities regarding professional oversight, competency, and support. I conclude that the transmission of the core values of multifaith engagement through multifaith supervision is an ethos worth striving for.

MULTIFAITH ENGAGEMENT: RESPECT FOR RELIGIOUS DIFFERENCE

The recognition of, and respect for, religious and spiritual differences is the key starting point in multifaith engagement. The multifaith movement, initiated in 1893 with the Parliament of World's Religions,[1] has sought to encourage harmony between global religious and spiritual communities toward their vision of "a world of peace, justice and sustainability."[2] However, multifaith engagement is rarely an easy endeavor. Socially progressive cosmopolitans[3] embrace the diversity, compassionate, and peace-building aspects of their religions; in contrast, anticosmopolitans tend to be reactionary, invoking religious freedoms to deny rights to others.[4] What is undeniable, in a world facing the twin challenges of secularization and globalization, is that "representatives of humankind's spiritual quest have been brought together in . . . an encounter so close that it leaves no room for retreat."[5]

Within Christianity, theological thinking about religions has traditionally categorized engagement as exclusivist, inclusivist, or pluralist.[6] However, Christocentric categories may serve a limited purpose:[7] it is possible "to affirm the spiritual paths of others in their own terms."[8] For example, the Church of England's "Presence and Engagement" program in the UK is committed to building bridges from its stance as "a reconciled and reconciling community"[9] within a multireligious society.

There have also been significant initiatives in the Muslim faith, particularly important in the light of the terrorist attacks of 9/11. The UAE hosted the first ever papal visit to the Arabian Peninsula

1. Halafoff, "Multifaith Movement," 35–54.
2. Parliament of the World's Religions, "Vision and Mission."
3. Kleingeld and Brown, "Cosmopolitanism." Cosmopolitans hold the worldview that all human beings are members of a single community.
4. Halafoff, *Interreligious Relations*, 2.
5. Bodhi, "Tolerance and Diversity," 1–3.
6. As defined by Francis X. Clooney: Exclusivist (Christ is the way, all must come to Christ); inclusivist (Christ is the way, but God is determined to save everyone, even far beyond the church, through Christ); pluralist (Christ is a way to God, but God saves other people in other ways as well). Clooney, "Theology, Dialogue, and Religious Others," 319.
7. Heim, "Crisscrossing the Rubicon," 688–90.
8. Drew, "Reconsidering the Possibility of Pluralism," 266.
9. Church of England, "Mission and Ministry," para. 18.

in 2019.[10] Writing as chair of the Institute of Islamic Thought in Washington, DC, Professor Sachedina proposes that "there is an inbuilt fundamental pluralism in Islam."[11] In recognizing "that there is no theological way to resolve religious differences,"[12] there is nonetheless a "prescription for living together in harmony and peace" offered by the Qur'an.[13] Leadership initiatives such as these demonstrate a clear willingness and theological mandate for multifaith engagement within the Muslim faith.

The Buddhist path avoids the extremes of fundamentalism (aggressive affirmation and proselytization) and spiritual universalism (that all religions espouse the same truth and ultimate liberation), summarized by Bhikkhu Bodhi as follows:

> True tolerance in religion involves the capacity to admit differences as real and fundamental, even as profound and unbridgeable, yet at the same time to respect the rights of those who follow a religion different from one's own (or no religion at all) to continue to do so without resentment, disadvantage or hindrance.[14]

Thus, recognizing and respecting religious differences is a key starting point in multifaith engagement. In the multifaith chaplaincy, this means learning how to reflect theologically about difference.

MULTIFAITH ENGAGEMENT: COOPERATION, MORALITY, COMMON GOALS

Respecting religious difference, whether between religious traditions or within one's own faith community, requires three conditions: intentional cooperation, a theological or moral mandate,

---

10. Al Jaber, "UAE Minister of State Hails Pope's Visit."
11. Sachedina, "Qur'anic Foundation of Interreligious Tolerance," 160.
12. Sachedina, "Qur'anic Foundation of Interreligious Tolerance," 160.
13. Sachedina, "Qur'anic Foundation of Interreligious Tolerance," 167.
14. Bodhi, "Tolerance and Diversity," para. 7.

and a clear understanding of common goals. However, there is nothing novel in this approach.

While the argument for the evolutionary basis for cooperation remains controversial, Tomasello[15] and others[16] posit that collaborative foraging shaped human cognition and communication such that "the interdependent engagement with others [became] central for successful functioning in social groups."[17] Recognizing our interdependence is key; we are effectively saying to each other, "I'm not going to be successful on my own—I have to stop and help you if I have an eye toward the future."[18]

As human groups started to expand, individuals no longer had personal relationships with all group members; group identity and culture emerged.[19] Human cooperation was thus based on the "moral judgments . . . necessary for determining the prosocial or negative status of cooperative interactions"[20] which ensured that the desired outcomes could be justified.

In modern times, organized religions and institutions of law uphold moral systems, the principles of which are largely consistent across human cultures.[21] Cooperation between religions can be facilitated when shared moral ground is uncovered and common goals are articulated, making "communication and collaboration possible and, indeed, indispensable for our times."[22] Multifaith spiritual care thus transmits strong messages about the worth and value of every human being: that meeting suffering with compassion is the universal moral and theological imperative.

15. Tomasello et al., "Evolution of Human Cooperation," 685.
16. Santos and West, "Coevolution of Cooperation and Cognition," 1–8.
17. Killen, Review of *Morality*, 326.
18. Tomasello, "Human Cooperation and Morality."
19. Tomasello, "Human Cooperation and Morality."
20. Killen, Review of *Morality*, 327.
21. Bentahila et al., "Universality and Cultural Diversity."
22. Schipani, "Exploration of Common Ground," 36.

SUPERVISION OF SPIRITUAL CARE PRACTITIONERS IN MULTIFAITH CONTEXTS

Supervision has the responsibility to ensure that spiritual care offered on a multifaith basis is a carefully considered endeavor. Multifaith spiritual care affects the practitioner in two ways: firstly, offering spiritual care to a person of a different faith tradition; secondly, working in a multifaith spiritual care team. Let us consider each of these aspects and the supervisory issues arising.

Firstly, in offering spiritual care to a person of a different faith tradition, the practitioner needs three attributes: to have a good awareness of the societal and institutional context in which that care is offered; a firm grounding in their own faith tradition; and competency around the professional and ethical limitations in their role. As a society of diverse cultures, Australia is committed to the right to freedom of thought, conscience, and religion or belief.[23] This is reflected in the aim of NSW Health to meet "the spiritual and religious needs of people of all faiths and people of no particular faith tradition"[24] on the basis that spiritual care is "integral to the process of healing and not . . . an addendum to other biomedical protocols."[25] The chaplaincy service within Corrective Services NSW offers a similarly broad approach in seeking to contribute to "the well-being, rehabilitation and reintegration of offenders."[26] Nongovernment religious providers in the aged care sector are not required to offer spiritual care on a multifaith basis; Uniting chooses to do so as a matter of policy.[27]

---

23. Attorney-General's Department, "Right to Freedom of Thought," para. 2.

24. NSW Health, "Memorandum of Understanding," 22. See Principle 1: The Nature of Healthcare Chaplaincy.

25. NSW Health, "Memorandum of Understanding," 22. See Principle 1: The Nature of Healthcare Chaplaincy.

26. Corrective Services NSW, "Chaplaincy Services," para. 1.

27. Uniting NSW.ACT, "Spiritual and Pastoral Care," para. 5. Uniting is a major Australian not-for-profit provider of a broad range of community services (such as in the aged care, disability, mental health, and youth sectors), built on the Christian foundations of the Uniting Church in Australia.

Whether the practitioner should engage in multifaith spiritual care depends on their theology and their competencies. Given "active proselytizing is not a function of... Pastoral Care Services,"[28] the practitioner needs to reflect theologically on difference so that they are sufficiently grounded in their own faith yet willing to respect and share the other's spiritual language and needs,[29] respecting "the power of language to disclose and obscure."[30] A key attribute for offering spiritual care to a person of a different faith (or no faith) is being able to relate as a fellow suffering human being, understanding the humanity we all have in common rather than perceiving a threat or a problem that could be solved if only the other person could get their theology and belief system sorted out. Humility, curiosity, and open-mindedness are qualities that go a long way toward meeting the other, as well as being able to identify when a referral is necessary—either because a specific religious or spiritual need has arisen, or because the practitioner has decided that, for ethical reasons, they no longer wish to continue offering spiritual care to the person in question.

Being grounded in their own faith, the practitioner, without "relativizing their own truth claims,"[31] requires a basic understanding of other faith traditions if they are to practice on a multifaith basis. The practitioner needs to demonstrate self-directed professional development, over and above clinical pastoral education, through academic study and/or involvement in organizations committed to multifaith practice such as Spiritual Care Australia[32] and Multifaith Chaplaincy.[33] Initiatives such as "Scriptural Reasoning" can serve as useful tools in "learning to disagree better"[34] through exploring sacred texts across faith boundaries. In an

28. NSW Health, "Memorandum of Understanding," 23. See Principle 4: The Needs of Patients and Families.
29. Cadge et al., "Training Chaplains and Spiritual Caregivers," 187–208.
30. Greider, "Religious Location and Counseling," 13.
31. Pesut et al., "Hospitable Hospitals in a Diverse Society," 832.
32. Spiritual Care Australia, "Vision, Mission and Values," paras. 1–6.
33. Multifaith Chaplaincy, "Our Process," para. 1.
34. Scriptural Reasoning, "Reflecting Together," para. 1.

increasingly secular society, it is to be hoped that "overarching spiritual languages and models"[35] will emerge from traditional religious language. Always with the objective of effective and ethical spiritual care, the practitioner needs to be able to communicate in a spiritual language that is meaningful to the other person.

Supervision thus has a responsibility to ensure that the supervisee understands the culture and expectations of their context and role; that they can articulate their spirituality and reflect upon their ability to communicate with people of different faiths; and that they understand their professional and ethical boundaries, and what to do when these boundaries have been, or are close to being, breached.

Let us consider the example of Terry, a Christian practitioner with many years of service in his parish and recently employed in an aged care facility as a pastoral practitioner. Terry was challenged by multifaith engagement in two ways. Firstly, he found it difficult to engage at more than a social level with residents of non-Christian faith (and including Christian denominations other than his own), assuming they "didn't have so much in common" and referring residents to a practitioner of their own specific faith outside the facility. Secondly, Terry struggled with the LGBTIQ+ activities offered within the facility, considering it "spiritual abuse" even though he had not heard any complaints from residents.

I supervised Terry as a CPE student doing a foundational CPE unit. We explored issues around Terry's pastoral identity, the scope of spiritual care, the role of religious interventions, and the policies of the aged care facility around inclusivity and tolerance. Using his good knowledge of the Bible, Terry started to reflect theologically on difference, articulating his personal mission and confirming his own faith identity as a Christian who could love his neighbor (Mark 12:31) and practice love in action (Rom 12:9–21). In addition, Terry set himself a learning goal which involved exploring the faith traditions of the residents he served. As Terry started to form closer spiritual relationships with all the residents he visited, he identified the appropriate times when professional

---

35. Zock, "Human Development and Pastoral Care," 449.

referrals were required, for instance, when an Orthodox resident requested the sacraments.

Furthermore, Terry discovered that he largely shared the ethos of the aged care facility in working to provide the best possible care for residents. While Terry's comfort level with the LGBTIQ+ activities did not change, he recognized that such activities were not forced on residents and that his discomfort was something he could tolerate without threatening the satisfaction he otherwise enjoyed in his role. Multifaith spiritual care thus emerged as an intentional and theologically motivated practice for Terry.

Working as part of a multifaith spiritual care team offers different opportunities and challenges for supervisees. The principles remain unchanged: cooperation grounded in one's own faith, respecting religious difference, and a firm eye on the common goal of alleviating human suffering. Successful multifaith teamwork is thus characterized by collaborative engagement rather than an exclusivist approach that avoids people who do not subscribe to one's religious views.

Collegiality across faiths is not always evident. Take the example of Marilyn, working as the only non-Christian chaplain in a large metropolitan hospital in NSW. Marilyn related how she had been sought out by a Christian chaplain in the team for their own spiritual support. This seemingly simple interaction was all the more significant in light of the workplace bullying she had endured at the start of her engagement a year previously, resulting in disciplinary action for the offending chaplain. Marilyn remained with the hospital, reflecting on and fortified by the wisdom and compassion teachings of the Brahma Viharas.[36] Over time, Marilyn's colleagues could see the effect of her calm and compassionate presence on patients and on themselves. Team relationships became more trusting and cooperative as this common goal was perceived. As a supervisor, Marilyn taught me how important it is

---

36. While the concept of the Brahma Viharas predates Buddhism, the Tevijjasutta (*Digha Nikaya* 13 of the Pāli Canon) demonstrates how the Buddha offers his unique interpretation of these four spiritual qualities (unconditional lovingkindness, compassion, altruistic joy, and equanimity).

to check in with supervisees on their working relationships with their colleagues, exploring difficulties and celebrating the success that comes with purposeful tolerance and goodwill.

Supervision has considerable responsibility in ensuring that multifaith spiritual care is not a foregone conclusion, rather an intentional activity that has been carefully considered by the spiritual care practitioner. Not only do they need to be firmly grounded in their own faith, they also need to be able to reflect theologically about difference, using meaningful spiritual language, always focused on effective spiritual care for the person they are serving.

MULTIFAITH SUPERVISION

Multifaith supervision transmits the intentional ethos of cooperation, morality, and seeking common goals in the compassionate service of the suffering human being. As a supervisor who practices in the tradition of the early Buddhism,[37] I continue to supervise spiritual care practitioners from multiple faith traditions. My goal is to assist the supervisee in becoming the most effective and compassionate spiritual care practitioner they can be, within the context of professional, safe, and ethical practice, and calling on their own faith for inspiration and mission. The supervisory contract is clearly delineated: my role is professional oversight and development in the context of the supervisee's learning goals; I make the explicit statement that I do not act as a spiritual director.

Some supervisees come to CPE with surprisingly little knowledge of their own faith. For example, June, a Christian practitioner, admitted that she had always struggled with theological reflection and did not know the Bible beyond a few well-known stories. To paraphrase Angela Merkel's lament, "the problem is too little Christianity."[38] My supervisory approach was to connect June with her Christian teachings, to guide her as she learned how to

---

37. Early Buddhism, associated with the Theravadin school, relies on the teachings given directly by the Buddha and his senior disciples as contained in the Pāli Canon.

38. O'Brien, "Secularism," 177.

use Christian Scripture as a resource for spiritual care, enabling her to uncover her own spiritual truths.

It is fair to say that some CPE students are suspicious and intolerant of an other-faith supervisor, perceiving a religious label rather than a person. Some students are blunt in their view that they have no time for a Buddhist supervisor, or that they feel unable to work with me because "Buddhists don't believe in God." I am grateful for their honesty and I do not argue with their preconceptions; rather I endeavor to model multifaith spiritual care in group supervision, invoking and naming the purposeful attitudes of patience, tolerance, and warmth that the students need to develop toward those they visit. Invariably, by the end of the unit, I have experienced respect in place of antagonism, acceptance in place of hostility. Within the context of CPE, I have found the majority of students have no issues with an other-faith supervisor. Indeed, a typical response came from Terry (who we met previously): as we were bringing our supervisory alliance to a close at the end of the CPE unit he reported, "I generally forgot you were Buddhist." When our egos get out of the way, the magic starts to happen.

Supervisees can be both challenged and affirmed when reflecting on how multifaith spiritual care might be offered. In presenting the same didactic to a variety of students, reactions have ranged from curiosity, inspiration, and challenge to downright insult and disgust. While the latter outcomes are not necessarily problematic, I have learned that well-established group trust and safety, through explicit contracting and deliberate time-tabling, better supports students to invoke an attitude of wondering and noticing and to adopt a stance of reflective practice rather than immediate reactivity. I consider that CPE is the perfect vehicle for attitudes and beliefs to be articulated and explored, the safety of both individual and group supervision a better arena than with a patient on a ward.

Moreover, I am alert to the fact that my own supervisors and co-supervisors may be equally challenged when we work together from different faith backgrounds and worldviews; what appears shocking to one maybe be deemed acceptable to the other.

I have found such experiences invariably useful; in contemplating the twin roadblocks of religious certitude and self-reliance (as proposed by Killen and de Beer[39]), the barriers to integration as a supervisor can be examined and reflected upon in the light of day.

Multifaith supervision confirms a genuine commitment to multifaith spiritual care, recognizing that spiritual paths will find expression in many different religious teachings in a religiously diverse and increasingly secular society. Guided by Buddhist principles that seek for peace, harmonious engagement, expressing unconditional lovingkindness, and enjoying the mutual benefits of spiritual friendship, I regard embodying the core values of multifaith engagement through the practice of multifaith supervision as the natural and joyful unfolding of my own spiritual journey, and an ethos worth striving for.

CONCLUSION

Having considered the foundational aspects of cooperation, morality, and common goals for multifaith engagement, I have explored the supervisory responsibilities that ensure spiritual care practitioners are spiritually, professionally, and ethically competent within their chosen context of practice. I have discussed how multifaith supervision follows the same paradigm of respect for theological difference in working toward the common goal of offering safe and effective spiritual care. As the transmission of the core values of multifaith engagement, I have concluded that multifaith supervision is an ethos worth striving for in today's increasingly diverse society.

BIBLIOGRAPHY

Al Jaber, Sultan Ahmed. "UAE Minister of State Hails Pope's Visit as Milestone Event." *Vatican News*, Feb. 1, 2019. https://www.vaticannews.va/en/pope/news/2019-02/pope-francis-uae.html.

---

39. Killen and de Beer, *Theological Reflection*, 168.

Attorney-General's Department. "Right to Freedom of Thought, Conscience and Religion or Belief." Public Sector guidance sheet. https://www.ag.gov.au/rights-and-protections/human-rights-and-anti-discrimination/human-rights-scrutiny/public-sector-guidance-sheets/right-freedom-thought-conscience-and-religion-or-belief.

Bentahila, Lina, et al. "Universality and Cultural Diversity in Moral Reasoning and Judgment." *Frontiers in Psychology* 12 (Dec. 2021). https://doi.org/10.3389/fpsyg.2021.764360.

Bodhi, Bhikkhu. "Tolerance and Diversity." *Buddhist Publication Society Newsletter* 24 (Summer/Fall 1993) 1–3. https://www.bps.lk/olib/nl/nl024-u.html.

Cadge, Wendy, et al. "Training Chaplains and Spiritual Caregivers: The Emergence and Growth of Chaplaincy Programs in Theological Education." *Pastoral Psychology* 69 (2020) 187–208.

Church of England. "The Church of England's Mission and Ministry in a Multi-Religious Society." June 2017. https://www.churchofengland.org/sites/default/files/2017-11/gs-2063-presence-and-engagement.pdf.

Clooney, Francis X. "Theology, Dialogue, and Religious Others: Some Recent Books in the Theology of Religions and Related Fields." *Religious Studies Review* 29 (2003) 319–27.

Corrective Services NSW. "Chaplaincy Services." https://correctiveservices.dcj.nsw.gov.au/reducing-re-offending/initiatives-to-support-offenders/health--safety-and-wellbeing/pastoral-care/chaplaincy-services.html.

Drew, Rose. "Reconsidering the Possibility of Pluralism." *Journal of Ecumenical Studies* 40 (2003) 245–66.

Greider, Kathleen J. "Religious Location and Counseling: Engaging Diversity and Difference in Views of Religion." In *Navigating Religious Difference in Spiritual Care and Counseling: Essays in Honor of Kathleen J. Greider*, edited by Jill L. Snodgrass, 11–44. Claremont, CA: Claremont, 2019.

Halafoff, Anna. *Interreligious Relations: Multifaith Movements and Critical Religious Pluralism: Precarity, Performativity and Peacebuilding.* Singapore: S. Rajaratnam School of International Studies, 2020.

———. "The Rise of the Multifaith Movement: 1893–1992." In *The Multifaith Movement: Global Risks and Cosmopolitan Solutions*, 35–54. Dordrecht, Netherlands: Springer, 2013.

Heim, S. Mark. "Crisscrossing the Rubicon: Reconsidering Religious Pluralism." *Christian Century* 108 (1991) 688–90.

Killen, Melanie. Review of *Morality: Cooperation Is Fundamental but It Is Not Enough to Ensure the Fair Treatment of Others*, by Michael Tomasello. *Human Development* 59 (2016) 324–37.

Killen, Patricia O'Connell, and John de Beer. *The Art of Theological Reflection.* New York: Crossroad, 1999.

Kleingeld, Pauline, and Eric Brown. "Cosmopolitanism." In *Stanford Encyclopedia of Philosophy*, edited by Edward N. Zalta. Article published

Feb. 23, 2002; revised Oct. 17, 2019. https://plato.stanford.edu/archives/win2019/entries/cosmopolitanism.

Liefbroer, Anke I., et al. "Interfaith Spiritual Care: A Systematic Review." *Journal of Religion and Health* 56 (2017) 1776–93.

Multifaith Chaplaincy. "Our Process." https://www.multifaithchaplaincy.org.au/about.

NSW Health. "NSW Health and Civil Chaplaincies Advisory Committee NSW Memorandum of Understanding: Attachment 4—Principles for Chaplaincy and Pastoral Care Services," 22–25. Policy directive, Jan. 19, 2011. https://www1.health.nsw.gov.au/pds/ActivePDSDocuments/PD2011_004.pdf.

O'Brien, Peter. "Secularism." In *The Muslim Question in Europe: Political Controversies and Public Philosophies*, 144–98. Philadelphia: Temple University Press, 2016.

Parliament of the World's Religions. "Our Vision and Mission." https://parliamentofreligions.org/our-work/mission.

Pesut, Barbara, et al. "Hospitable Hospitals in a Diverse Society: From Chaplains to Spiritual Care Providers." *Journal of Religion and Health* 51 (2012) 825–36.

Sachedina, Abdulaziz. "The Qur'anic Foundation of Interreligious Tolerance." In *Fine Differences: The Al-Alwani Muslim-Christian Lectures 2010-2017*, edited by Richard J. Jones, 160–74. Herndon, VA: International Institute of Islamic Thought, 2020.

Santos, Miguel dos, and Stuart A. West. "The Coevolution of Cooperation and Cognition in Humans." *Proceedings of The Royal Society B: Biological Sciences* 285 (2018) 20180723. https://doi.org/10.1098/rspb.2018.0723.

Schipani, Daniel S. "An Exploration of Common Ground in Pastoral and Spiritual Care: Religious Community, Human Spirit, Wisdom, and Creative Imagination." In *Care, Healing, and Human Well-Being Within Interreligious Discourses*, edited by Helmut Weiss et al., 36–50. Stellenbosch, South Africa: African Sun Media, 2021.

Scriptural Reasoning. "Reflecting Together on Sacred Texts." http://www.scripturalreasoning.org.

Spiritual Care Australia. "Our Vision, Mission and Values." https://www.spiritualcareaustralia.org.au/about-us/who-we-are.

Tomasello, Michael. "A Lecture in Psychology: Origins of Human Cooperation and Morality." Annual Reviews, Aug. 10, 2012. YouTube video. https://www.youtube.com/watch?v=rOHxsZBD3Us.

Tomasello, Michael, et al. "Two Key Steps in the Evolution of Human Cooperation: The Interdependence Hypothesis." *Current Anthropology* 53 (2012) 673–92.

Uniting NSW.ACT. "Spiritual and Pastoral Care." https://www.uniting.org/community-impact/spiritual-care.

Wikipedia. "Cosmopolitanism." Last modified Oct. 7, 2022. https://en.wikipedia.org/wiki/Cosmopolitanism.

Zock, Hetty. "Human Development and Pastoral Care in a Postmodern Age: Donald Capps, Erik H. Erikson, and Beyond." *Journal of Religion and Health* 57 (2018) 437–50.

4

Reflective Spaces, Liberating Spaces

How the Three Doors of Liberation Teaching Provides a Framework for Buddhist Supervisors to Deepen Their Reflective Work with Students

DEBRA KELLY

> Freedom in Zen is not having more options.
> Freedom is being nobody going nowhere.[1]
> —GEOFF DAWSON

> What is freedom?
> It is the moment-by-moment experience of not being run by one's own reactive mechanisms.[2]
> —KEN MCLEOD

---

1. Dawson, "Ordinary Mind Zen School."
2. McLeod, "Freedom and Choice."

INTRODUCTION

As part of the clinical pastoral education accreditation process, provisional pastoral supervisors are asked to explore how their spiritual framework "informs, enlightens and/or challenges"[3] their work and supervisory identity. I have read many articles by Buddhist writers on embodied listening and compassionate presence, but when I came across the "Three Doors of Liberation," I was intrigued. Could this ancient teaching provide a useful framework for reflective work in supervision, and might it offer a complementary perspective on current Western models?

In this chapter, I will outline the Three Doors of Liberation[4] teaching and show how it has deepened my understanding of what happens in reflective supervisory spaces. The Three Doors have been translated from the Sanskrit as *emptiness, signlessness,* and *aimlessness* by Vietnamese Zen teacher Thích Nhât Hanh,[5] who says that contemplating them can help us cut through dualistic notions of good and bad, right and wrong, and recognize our true nature. When we see our true nature, which he calls *interbeing*, we can drop our self-centered preoccupations and be free of the endless struggle for self-improvement (which includes unhelpful attachment to spiritual goals). For Buddhists, the Three Doors reveal the freedom inherent in the true nature of phenomena (emptiness), the freedom in relating to the world without concepts (signlessness), and the freedom found in the present moment (aimlessness). All three are aspects of the same reality and they interpenetrate and presuppose each other.

---

3. NSWCCPE, "Paper Three: The Applicant's Theological/Spiritual Worldview," sec. 9.5.2.5 in *Handbook* (on the formation and accreditation of clinical pastoral supervisors).

4. Sanskrit: *trivimoksamukha* (Three Doors of Liberation, also known as the Three Concentrations). The teaching appears in the *Treatise on the Liberations of the Patisambhidāmagga* and the *Visuddhimagga* (latter approximately fifth century CE) and other sources. For more commentary see Thích Nhât Hanh, "Discourse on the Dharma Seal."

5. Thích Nhât Hanh (1926–2022) was a Vietnamese Zen monk, teacher, author, and peace activist during the Vietnam war, who clarified Buddhist teachings without over-simplification.

EMPTINESS

> The failure to understand emptiness keeps people enthralled by the stories the mind fabricates as it wanders in a trance of hallucinated narratives.[6]
>
> —Shaila Catherine

> [Stay] empty and unknowing, uncluttered by premature judgment, theory, and interpretation.[7]
>
> —Wilfred Bion

Thích Nhất Hanh said the first door of liberation, emptiness[8] (having no-self), is a "description of reality."[9] It is not the same as nonexistence; rather it means that all things exist *only in relation to everything else*.[10] For example, if we look at a specific combination of metal, plastic, glass, and rubber, we see a truck, but a "truck" is just a concept we project onto this particular assembly of things. There is no inherent "truck essence" in the metal, plastic, glass, or rubber. A person, likewise, is made up entirely of "non-self" elements (culture, parents, education, experiences, food), and if you take these away, nothing else remains. Emptiness says this is true

---

6. Catherine, *Focused and Fearless*, 211.

7. Bion, *Learning from Experience*.

8. The Sanskrit word *śūnyatā* (emptiness, voidness) refers to the teaching that all things are empty of intrinsic existence, notably developed by Nāgārjuna in the second century CE. O'Brien, "What Do Buddhist Teachings Mean?" In his foreword to *A Profound Mind* by the Dalai Lama, Tibetan monk Nicholas Vreeland writes, "The chief difference between Buddhism and the world's other major faith traditions lies in its presentation of our core identity. The existence of the soul or self . . . is not only firmly denied . . . ; belief in it is identified as the source of all our misery." Dalai Lama, *Profound Mind*, ix.

9. Thích Nhất Hanh, "What Are the Three Doors."

10. The Buddhist view of personhood is that humans are composed of *skandhas* (bundles) consisting of physical form, feelings/sensations, perceptions, mental formations, and consciousness, all in constant flux. O'Brien, "Five Skandhas."

of all phenomena, and that everything exists co-independently and impermanently.[11]

Far from being a negative teaching, by virtue of not clinging to a separate identity, emptiness sees the potentiality in all things, in which lies the basis for hope. Whereas holding on to a false separateness—identifying every thought, feeling and wish with the "I" concept—causes humans to suffer, emptiness connects us beyond personality.[12]

As a supervisor, I am asked to develop my pastoral identity, yet, according to Buddhist thought, my identity is insubstantial. This could be problematic were it not for the fact that CPE literature essentially supports a view of supervisory spaces as being unfixed and fluid entities in which experience, not knowledge, best informs us. Lois Zachary, for instance, says that in supervision "we sit at the feet of our experience; we allow our work to become our teacher."[13]

Below is an excerpt from the most popular Mahāyāna[14] text, the heart sutra.[15]

---

11. The teaching of "dependent origination" states that all things are interconnected, and nothing is permanent. To learn more, see https://tricycle.org/beginners/buddhism/dependent-origination.

12. Tart, *States of Consciousness*, 23. Psychologist Charles Tart regards personality as no more than "psychic automatism" consisting of "automatic, egocentric, habit-determined patterns of thought, emotive reaction and assessment, and imaginary activity that filter and distort reality and skew behaviour, according to the needs of the self-project."

13. Zachary, *Mentor's Guide*, 13.

14. *Mahāyāna* (greater vehicle) refers to the branch of Buddhism that arose in India around the first century CE and became the dominant form in Central and East Asia by the ninth century. It is now found primarily in China, Taiwan, Vietnam, Japan, and Korea. Zen is a Mahāyāna school of Buddhism, influenced by Chinese and Japanese traditions such as Taoism. *Theravāda* (the way of the elders) refers to early Indian Buddhism, now found in Sri Lanka, Thailand, Burma, and Laos. A third branch is Tibetan *Vajrayāna* (diamond vehicle) Buddhism. Nalanda, "Buddhist Traditions."

15. A copy of the heart sutra, Sanskrit, *Prajñāpāramitāhrdaya* (The Heart of the Perfection of Wisdom), was found dated 661 CE. Authorship is unknown. DharmaNet, "Heart Sutra."

> From the depths of prajñā wisdom, the Bodhisattva of Compassion
> Saw into the emptiness of every construct
> And so passed beyond all suffering.
> Know then, that in such depths,
> Form is only emptiness, emptiness only form.
> Form is emptiness, emptiness is form . . .
>
> . . . The Bodhisattva who dwells in this perfect wisdom, attaining nothing,
> Is not entrapped by delusive fantasies
> And where there are no such obstacles, there can be no fear.[16]

In meditation, it is possible to experience "the emptiness of every construct" directly. As well as relaxing the body and soothing the mind, awareness of breathing[17] allows us to rest in the consciousness behind our thinking and emotional processes, or the "gaps between thoughts." By observing the machinations of the mind (and our individual patterns of conditioning) from a clearer perspective, we come to see that thoughts are "mental events" rather than truths and we see the benefits of letting go of our likes, dislikes, and other fixations before they do harm. Buddhist psychologist John Welwood explains, "Through sitting quietly with ourselves, we see how we are constantly trying to maintain our identity, how our thoughts act as a kind of glue that holds our identity structure together."[18] Sustained awareness loosens this structure so we can sense the larger ground, which is our interconnected nature.

Helpfully, the mechanics of breathing provide an illustration of emptiness as the diaphragm contracts as we breath in and expands/relaxes as we breath out. Contraction of the body occurs in everyday life when we want something to happen, or we are resisting something that is happening, whereas relaxation is a letting go. In reflective spaces, even a momentary pause provides an

---

16. Ordinary Mind Zen School Sydney, "Prajna Paramita Heart Sutra."

17. In Zen, breath awareness and/or counting is used as a focus, particularly at the beginning of a meditation or for novices.

18. Welwood, *Psychology of Awakening*, 31.

opportunity for us to notice the contraction in our bodies and, restraining from "*quick, routine responses*,"[19] sink into the background flow of awareness. When connected to our true nature (which is always equanimous) our responses need not come from a place of tension and hurt.

Students of CPE must manage their own emotional responses as well as holding those of the patient, and these emotions often resurface in supervision. Reflective inquiry can provide the environment in which compulsions to know, to fix, and to achieve lose their energy. In confronting their raw edges and vulnerability, the student begins to question what they thought they knew.

In his essay "You Learn It in Your Heart," Logan C. Jones states that transformation is a process of becoming aware of "how and why the structure of psycho-cultural assumptions has come to constrain the way we see ourselves and our relationships."[20] Supervision provides an opportunity to work with these assumptions and default responses by facilitating the reflective space in which our subconscious motives may emerge. Understanding context is crucial because when we appreciate where the student is coming from, and where we are coming from, we naturally have more empathy, not just as a supervisory stance but as an appreciation of the suffering that results in defending unhelpful core beliefs. Seeing the illusory nature of thought allows us to question the assumptions that support the false self and recognize some of the unhelpful causes and conditions that contribute to who we are. It is a powerful tool to cut through delusion and can lead to a healthy sense of disillusionment with the mind's endless commentary—especially when such self-centered activity is seen to cause unnecessary suffering. This reinforces Zen teacher Dōgen Zenji's often quoted statement "When we study the self, we forget the self."[21]

19. Hewson and Carroll invite us to "pause and notice" as part of the "Mindful Stance" in *Reflective Practice in Supervision*, 159.

20. Jones, "You Learn It in Your Heart."

21. From Eihei Dōgen's essay "Genjo Kōan" (Actualizing the Fundamental Point) in his book *Shōbōgenzō* (True Dharma Eye Treasury). Dōgen lived in thirteenth-century Japan and founded the Soto Zen school. Dōgen, *Shōbōgenzō*, 31.

Emptiness reminds us that we are all made up of myriad causes and conditions, including culture, birth family, education, formators, and life experiences. This allows us to meet our students with curious compassion as they make meaning of their encounters and explore what gets in the way of them being wholly present. We see them relax as they realize CPE is a safe place to share feelings of discomfort and uncertainty, even failure. In this way, emptiness supports the work that happens in liminal supervisory spaces.

SIGNLESSNESS

Dizang was a Zen teacher who decided to quiz his student:

> Dizang asked Fayan, "Where are you going?"
>
> Fayan said, "Around on pilgrimage."
>
> Dizang said, "What is the purpose of pilgrimage?"
>
> Fayan said, "I don't know."
>
> Dizang said, "Not knowing is most intimate."[22]

The second door of liberation is signlessness[23] (having no form), which holds that phenomena seem to possess certain qualities but they are mentally imputed and not part of the objects they describe. This teaching frees us from getting caught in an abstract way of relating to the world. Labels might be helpful in a laboratory or a pantry but when we conceptualize our world (which humans naturally tend to do) we fixate on certain things and do not see people or situations clearly; we confuse the world as it is defined and measured with the world as it *actually is*.[24] Unfortu-

---

22. This exchange appears in Case 20 of the *Book of Equanimity*, which contains 100 *kōans*, or Zen teaching riddles, written by Chan teacher Hongzhi Zhengiue (1091–1157). Wick, *Book of Equanimity*, 63.

23. Sanskrit, *animittā* (signlessness, nonceptual proliferation).

24. Welwood, *Psychology of Awakening*, 51. John Welwood likens the

nately, when we accept our perceptions as truth, we construct rigid opinions and beliefs around them which we must then defend, unleashing all sorts of trouble. Thus, Seng Can's urging, "Do not search for truth; only cease to cherish opinions."[25]

Real life is messy, brutal, unpredictable, and unfair as well as amazing and beautiful and miraculous. Fayan knew that adopting an open and curious "don't know mind"[26] gets to the heart of what it means to experience life fully. When we know something—or think we know—our ego identity[27] imposes itself, but when we do not know, experience reveals itself. For Thích Nhât Hanh, the hallmark of such a mind is freedom. He challenges us: "For things to reveal themselves to us, we need to be ready to abandon our views about them."[28]

In everyday life, pausing at the primary feeling (hurt, anger, shock) *before* conceptualization takes place is psychologically possible but very rarely practiced, because humans are driven by unconscious conditioning and a love of drama. The invitation in reflective inquiry is to "pause and notice" the messages conveyed in ourselves and others *before* conceptualization has taken place and not to allow mental proliferation to occur. Energy usually spent on

---

mind's tendency to grasp onto solid forms to a bird in flight which is always looking for the next branch to land on instead of enjoying flying through the air. When we continually look for a "belief, attitude, identity or emotional reaction to hold onto," we miss "the interplay of form and emptiness in the mindstream—out of which all creativity arises."

25. Seng Can was the third Chan patriarch of Chinese Buddhism and lived around the fifth century CE. Authorship of this quote has been disputed. Seng-ts'an, "Verses on the Faith Mind."

26. This paraphrase of "beginner's mind" was coined by Korean Zen Master Seung Sahn, many years after Fayan. Providence Zen Center, *Only Don't Know*. Similarly, "beginner's mind" is a phrase used by Japanese Zen priest Shunryu Suzuki in his classic *Zen Mind, Beginner's Mind*. See his prologue.

27. Welwood, *Psychology of Awakening*, 44. Welwood thinks that children need to develop an ego—in the Freudian sense—to help them function in the world, however, whereas Freud saw the ego as "an indispensable mental structure," Buddhists see it as "an activity, created moment by moment and therefore dispensable." Welwood adds, "Ego is awareness in a contracted state; egolessness is the open spacious ground of being."

28. Thích Nhât Hanh, *Being Peace*, 48.

emotional reactivity and ego-defense is then available for attentive presence and insight. Psychotherapist Hubert Benoit says that this requires "an effort of de-contraction—a non-action opposed to our reflex inner agitation."[29] It's an exhale, then, not an inhale.

My favorite teaching on this tentative stance is from Jain[30] philosophy, consisting of the linked theories of *anekāntavāda* (many sidedness), *syādvāda* (let's wait and see), and *ahimsa* (non-harming). *Anekāntavāda* holds that our approaches to understanding reality are inevitably partial and limited, therefore our need to be right is not logical. Whatever stance we take, we must keep in mind that others may have perceived what we, ourselves, have not. For example, how we recognize what is sacred for us may be our individual truth, but (the theory states) it is just one aspect of the truth. The Indian parable of the elephant and the five blind men[31] charmingly illustrates this teaching. The second concept, *syādvāda*, holds that because there are an almost infinite number of ways to describe an event or experience, we must seriously consider other points of view. This leads to the third concept, *ahimsa* (non-harming), being manifested in humility, respect, and kindness.

One way in which signlessness influences my supervisory foundation is that I do not assume mine to be the only path. If I see my view as just a view (not truth) I will not be so attached to that view. Thus, the Buddha discovered an effective method of liberation from suffering, but it is not the only model. Apart from the fact that a person's religion is largely a matter of where they are born, many other causes and conditions play a part, with constructivist learning theory reminding us that knowledge is not "out there" but assembled by individual learners and mediated

29. Benoit, *Zen*, 91.

30. Jainism and Buddhism began as Hindu offshoots around the fifth century BCE, and they share many teachings in common. Jains take the precept of non-harming (*ahimsa*) to the extreme. Unacademy, "Jainism and Buddhism."

31. In the story of the blind men and the elephant, each man believes that what he touches reveals the true nature of the object. Hence, one touches the elephant's tail and declares it is a whip, another a leg and says it is a pillar, another an ear and says it is a fan, and so on.

through cultural symbols and language.[32] Our worldview necessarily shapes the questions we ask and therefore the answers we find, while ultimate truth, which represents a particular culture, time, and place, transcends doctrine.

Signlessness helps us to step into the student's world with more humility and to consider when our theories and opinions interfere with learning. We are called to look beyond the surface to see the students express their "connection to their wholeness."[33] Just like a gardener who can see the vegetables that are yet to grow in the seed and compost, so can the supervisor see beyond appearances to the student's true nature. Recognizing and confirming (though our presence) the student's true nature as none other than the ground of all being, the supervisor's compassionate holding allows the student to come back to this ground. Like Carl Rogers's "nondirective" approach in counseling,[34] signlessness supports the student as they find their own sources of wisdom.

AIMLESSNESS

"The more we do Zen Practice, the less clever we become, the less successful we become, the less spiritually advanced we become. Out of this poverty of Spirit we mature in practice."[35]

—GEOFF DAWSON

The third door, aimlessness[36] (having no agenda), means living our lives as they are happening, rather than living psychologically in the past or the future. Aimlessness does not mean being lazy or disorganized; we still have our plans and our goals, and we

---

32. Vygotsky, *Mind in Society*.
33. Gabriel, "Implications for Interfaith Chaplaincy," 94.
34. de Vos and Braam, "Humanist Chaplains."
35. Dawson, "Ordinary Mind Zen School."
36. Sanskrit, *apranihita* (aimlessness or literally "placing nothing in front").

still try our best, but like the lilies in the field, who "neither toil nor spin,"[37] our "purpose" is simply to be fully alive.

Living according to aimlessness releases the craving for things to turn out a certain way, which is the flip side of not accepting what is happening now (humans have a poor record of predicting what will make us happy anyway). Students are often challenged to be present with whatever the patient is presenting because they feel helpless in the face of suffering, but it could be argued that in the present moment there is nothing to fear, only something to deal with.[38] Thus, aimlessness emphasizes the preeminence of compassionate presence over knowing what to do or say. Similarly, in supervisory spaces, our plans for the student hover in the background but they are not the focus. Instead, skillful reflective questions encourage the student to stay in the present and sit in wondering and not knowing.

Thích Nhât Hanh describes this process thus:

> We recognize internal knots and latent tendencies
> So we can transform them.
> When our habit energies dissipate,
> Transformation at the base is there.
> The present moment contains past and future.
> The secret of transformation is in the way we handle this very moment.[39]

Present moment awareness involves both embodiment and attentiveness. Firstly, somatic awareness is a shortcut to the present moment and a reliable ally when working with emotions. Secondly, attentiveness (which involves a level of concentration and nonreactivity toward external and internal stimuli) facilitates what some call sacred space and others liminality.[40] Martin Buber suggests that when two people are completely present to each

---

37. Luke 12:27 NRSV.
38. Fischer, *When You Greet Me*, 293.
39. Thích Nhât Hanh, "Path of Practice," 222.
40. Liminality: (Latin: threshold) a transitional state from one stage to the next which, if safely traversed, brings freedom and relief. Le Hunte, "Liminality," para. 1.

other and there is "mutuality, directness, presentness, intensity and ineffability,"[41] the relationship itself is healing, which seems true. Aimlessness helps us offer this authentic presence to our students. Buddhist writer Rodney Smith writes, "When all states of mind are met with acceptance, much of the projected discomfort with the world ends and the polarities of life are set aside for the common integrity of the whole. This is the beginning of effort toward nonduality and interconnectedness."[42]

CONCLUSION

In this chapter I have shown how the Three Doors of Liberation teaching adds a deeper dimension to my reflective practice with students, promoting the two strands of Buddhist practice: wisdom and compassion. Emptiness, signlessness, and aimlessness together describe a life worth living, a psychologically healthy life in which we are aware and awake, connected to others and open to the freshness of lived experience. Michael Carroll reminds us that supervision is "always about the quality of awareness."[43] It is this awareness that allows us to recognize the false self and come to rest in our true nature, to invite nonconceptual wisdom instead of attaching to theories and dualistic notions, and to relax into the present moment. In this way, practicing the Three Doors of Liberation facilitates the possibility of true intimacy and radical transformation in our personal and supervisory relationships, freeing us to be who we really are.

BIBLIOGRAPHY

Benoit, Hubert. *Zen and the Psychology of Transformation: The Supreme Doctrine*. Revised ed. Rochester, VT: Inner Traditions International, 1990.

Bion, Wilfred. *Learning from Experience*. London: Karnac, 1984.

41. Martin and Cowan, "Remembering Martin Buber."
42. Smith, *Stepping Out of Self Deception*, 93.
43. Carroll, "Supervision: Critical Reflection," 13.

Carroll, Michael. "From Mindless to Mindful Practice: On Learning Reflection in Supervision." *Psychotherapy in Australia* 15 (2009) 40–51.

———. "Supervision: Critical Reflection for Transformational Learning (Part 2)." *Clinical Supervisor* 29 (2010) 1–19.

Catherine, Shaila. *Focused and Fearless: A Meditator's Guide to States of Deep Joy, Calm, and Clarity*. Boston, MA: Wisdom, 2008.

Connolly, Ben. *Inside Vasubandhu's Yogacara: A Practitioner's Guide*. Somerville, MA: Wisdom. 2016.

Dalai Lama [Tenzin Gyatso]. *A Profound Mind. Cultivating Wisdom in Everyday Life*. Edited by Nicholas Vreeland. New York: Harmony Books, 2011.

Dawson, Geoff. "The Gentle Art of Pausing." *Ordinary Mind Zen School*. Feb. 20, 2024. Podcast. https://soundcloud.com/ordinarymind/the-gentle-art-of-pausing.

———. "Ordinary Mind Zen School (OMZS)." Zen Chat member newsletter, edited by Althea Reid, Feb. 15, 2024.

de Vos, Jeroen, and Arjan W. Braam. "An Empirical Study on the Nature of the Verbal Responses of Humanist Chaplains." *Religions* 12 (Dec. 2021) 1080. https://www.mdpi.com/2077-1444/12/12/1080.

DharmaNet. "The Heart Sutra." https://dharmanet.org/heart-sutra-2.

Dōgen, Eihei. *Shōbōgenzō: The Treasure House of the Eye of the True Teachings, A Trainee's Translation of Great Master Dōgen's Spiritual Masterpiece*. Translated by Hubert Nearman. Mount Shasta, CA: Shasta Abbey, 2007.

Fischer, Norman. *When You Greet Me I Bow: Notes and Reflections from a Life in Zen*. New York: Shambhala, 2021.

Franks, Anne, and John Meteyard. "Liminality: The Transforming Grace of In-Between Places." *Journal of Pastoral Care and Counseling* 61 (2007) 215–22.

Gabriel, Victor. "Implications for Interfaith Chaplaincy from a Tibetan Buddhist Understanding of Religious Location and the Two Truths." In *Navigating Religious Difference in Spiritual Care and Counseling: Essays in Honor of Kathleen J. Greider*, edited by Jill L. Snodgrass, 87–98. Claremont, CA: Claremont, 2019.

Hewson, Daphne, and Michael Carroll. *Reflective Practice in Supervision*. Hazelbrook, Australia: Moshpit, 2016.

Jones, Logan C. "You Learn It in Your Heart: Transformative Learning Theory and Clinical Pastoral Education." *Journal of Pastoral Care and Counseling* 64 (2010) 1–10.

Le Hunte, Bem. "Liminality." In *The Palgrave Encyclopedia of the Possible*, edited by Vlad Petre Glăveneau. Cham, Switzerland: Palgrave Macmillan, 2022. https://doi.org/10.1007/978-3-319-98390-5_246-1.

Martin, Matthew, and Eric W. Cowan. "Remembering Martin Buber and the I–Thou in Counseling." *Counseling Today* (May 2019). https://www.counseling.org/publications/counseling-today-magazine/article-archive/article/legacy/remembering-martin-buber-and-the-i-thou-in-counseling.

Maslow, Abraham H. *Motivation and Personality*. 2nd ed. New York: Harper and Row, 1970.
McLeod, Ken. "Freedom and Choice: Breaking Free from the Tyranny of Reaction." *Tricycle* (Winter 2012). https://tricycle.org/magazine/freedom-and-choice.
Nalanda. "Buddhist Traditions." July 1, 2012. https://www.nalanda.org.my/buddhist-traditions.
Novak, Philip. "Attention." In *Encyclopedia of Religion*. Vol. 1. Edited by Mircea Eliade and Charles J. Adams, 501–9. New York: Macmillan, 1987.
NSWCCPE. *Handbook*. Rev. Oct. 2024. https://files.milbel.com.au/file/milbel-site-public/site_data/nswccpe.edu.au/20241113_093755_dc0db6ed_Website_version_Handbook_2024_v5.pdf.
O'Brien, Barbara. "The Five Skandhas: An Introduction to the Aggregates." Learn Religions, Dec. 21, 2018. https://www.learnreligions.com/the-skandhas-450192.
———. "What Do Buddhist Teachings Mean by Sunyata, or Emptiness?" Learn Religions, June 26, 2019. https://www.learnreligions.com/sunyata-or-emptiness-450191.
Ordinary Mind Zen School Sydney. "The Prajna Paramita Heart Sutra." https://zensydney.com/The-Prajna-Paramita-Heart-Sutra.
Providence Zen Center. *Only Don't Know: Selected Teaching Letters of Zen Master Seung Sahn*. Edited by Hyon Gak Sunim. Boston: Shambhala, 1999. https://terebess.hu/zen/mesterek/Seung-Sahn-Only-Don-t-Know.pdf.
Seng-ts'an, Chien-chih. "Verses on the Faith Mind." Translated by Richard B. Clarke. https://terebess.hu/english/hsin.html#3.
Smith, Rodney. *Stepping Out of Self Deception: The Buddha's Teaching of No-Self*. New York: Shambhala, 2016.
Suzuki, Shunryu. *Zen Mind, Beginner's Mind*. Boulder, CO: Shambhala, 2006.
Tart, Charles T. *States of Consciousness*. New York: E. P. Dutton, 1975.
Thích Nhât Hanh. *Being Peace*. New York: Random House, 2005.
———, trans. "Discourse on the Dharma Seal and the Three Doors of Liberation." Plum Village. https://plumvillage.org/library/sutras/discourse-on-the-dharma-seal-the-three-doors-of-liberation.
———. *The Heart of the Buddha's Teaching*. New York: Harmony, 1998.
———. "The Path of Practice." In *Transformation at the Base*, 197–245. Berkeley, CA: Parallax, 2001.
———. "Thich Nhat Hanh's Doors of Liberation: No Self, No Form, No Goal." Lion's Roar, Mar. 31, 2022. https://www.lionsroar.com/thich-nhat-hanh-doors-of-liberation.
———. "Thich Nhat Hanh: What Are the Three Doors of Liberation." Awaken, Oct. 23, 2021. https://awaken.com/2021/10/what-are-the-three-doors-of-liberation.
Unacademy. "Similarities and Differences Between Jainism and Buddhism." https://unacademy.com/content/bpsc/study-material/history/similarities-and-differences-between-jainism-and-buddhism.

Vygotsky, L. S. *Mind in Society: The Development of Higher Psychological Processes.* Cambridge, MA: Harvard University Press, 1978.

Welwood, John. *The Psychology of Awakening.* Boston: Shambhala, 2002.

Wick, Gerry Shishin. *The Book of Equanimity: Illuminating Classic Zen Koans.* Somerville, MA: Wisdom, 2005.

Zachary, Lois J. *The Mentor's Guide: Facilitating Effective Learning Relationships.* Hoboken, NJ: Jossey-Bass, 2000.

5

Academic Excellence and Diversity in CPE Supervision

PETER POWELL

INTRODUCTION

A critical element in training supervisors in the standards of the Australia and New Zealand Association for Clinical Pastoral Education is the development and maintenance of measurable standards emphasizing academic and pastoral excellence. A review of standards reveals a focus on reading and writing, including the ability to present reports, case studies, and final evaluations. In New South Wales, Australia, CPE programs are linked to the Sydney College of Divinity, a University College, including a master's degree program. This approach is essentially different to the origins of the action-reflection learning methodology that underpins CPE, originating with Anton Boisen. At that time, in the early 1920s, the emphasis was on attention to the story revealed in the patient in a mental health setting, the *living human document*.[1] While no less rigorous in its action-reflection methodology than subsequent evolving programs, the emphasis was on pastoral

---

1. Gulo, "Living Human Document," 141–43.

practice and the pastoral relationship rather than the academic demands that came later. This chapter will raise questions regarding the dominant Western, privileged culture surrounding CPE while challenging CPE educators to consider greater inclusion of those from nonliterary and colonized cultures. This requires designing alternate educational pathways that are shaped by alternative narratives while maintaining supervisory and educational excellence.

DISSONANCE BETWEEN CULTURAL AWARENESS AND REGULATIONS

The latest ANZACPE standards approved in 2022 define CPE as

> education and formation for the professional work of pastoral/spiritual care. CPE uses an educational methodology that combines knowledge of theology/spirituality (what we believe), with knowledge of education (how we learn), with knowledge of the behavioural sciences (who we are as human beings). CPE's methodology utilizes the *"action-reflection"* model of learning. The *"action"* component entails practical experience in the work of pastoral/spiritual care within a pastoral/spiritual care setting; this care acknowledges and attends to the human condition, particularly life's spiritual dimensions. The *"reflection"* component entails the exploration, articulation and integration of the pastoral/spiritual carer's experience, the dynamics present, and the theological/spiritual implications. This *"action-reflection"* process is integral to CPE students'/participants' understanding and the formation of their pastoral/spiritual care identity and competence. CPE encourages learning from the *"living human documents."* The specific content of a CPE Unit will depend upon the particular interests and needs of the students.[2]

Having provided this relational, action-reflection definition, the standards then go on to develop an assessment process heavily dependent upon written skills. While the standards occasionally

2. *ANZACPE Standards*, 1.

refer to a more flexible assessment process namely, *written/visual/ oral form*, those references appeared to be an obligatory cultural concession, rather than an integrated process. For example, in lines 46 and 47 it states:

> Each CPE student/participant is required to present within the learning group at least eight of the above written/visual/oral materials for peer supervision and supervisor feedback.[3]

However, the standards continue in lines 48 and 49 to say:

> Student/participants may be asked to *complete other papers*, presentations and learning journals as required (my italics).[4]

These contradictions continue throughout the regulations. It would appear to demonstrate a commitment by the Association to be culturally sensitive and relevant without the necessary discipline of exploring how that can be carried through and assessed. Note some of the key themes articulated within the regulations such as engage in pastoral/spiritual care with a variety of people with their unique experiences, take into account their individual cultural/spiritual/social backgrounds, listen reflectively, initiate pastoral/spiritual relationships, engage with interdisciplinary staff, function ethically, and articulate assumptions, attitudes, and values. Two things can be quickly identified:

1. The regulations are describing an interpersonal, relational pastoral practice. There is nothing in these descriptions that articulates the necessity for that activity to be assessed in written form and yet references to written form continue to appear throughout the regulations.

2. The historical beginnings of CPE can be seen in the reference to "interdisciplinary staff." This assumes some form of formal institution, not necessarily relevant to CPE, particularly in Aboriginal or Pacific peoples contexts. (Here I speak of

---

3. *ANZACPE Standards*, 2.
4. *ANZACPE Standards*, 2.

primary themes. Not all Aboriginal or Pacific people process learning in exactly the same way.)

CULTURAL AWARENESS DOES NOT GUARANTEE CULTURALLY SENSITIVE PROCESSES

In New Zealand there is a noticeable awareness of cultural diversity and sensitivity to Māori people. On many occasions I have been struck by how many supervisors have faithfully learned a variety of greetings and rituals and presented them fluently in the Māori language. There is no equivalent process in Australia, although it needs to be noted that there are hundreds of First Nations languages in Australia and not all are intact.

What stands out in the regulations—and in the general practice of CPE in Australia—is an awareness of cultural diversity coupled with a lack of development of appropriate cultural educational and assessment processes. Western, linear thinking still dominates. Some of the language reflects a colonial elitism, removing it from the necessary process required to explore and listen to the living human documents in non-Western cultures.

Referring to Boisen, Robert Leas writes:

> He believed in the first-hand study of human experience as a way to challenge seminarians to think theologically. What he called reading "the living human documents" was a necessary supplement to classroom training in the seminary experience. In 1926, he wrote about his method, "Theological training for the future will be a continuous affair, with the parish as the laboratory and a person with need the main concern, and the seminary a 'clearing-house' of theological tradition and formation and the supervisor of methods. The attention will be shifted from the past to the present; from books to the raw material of life."[5]

---

5. Leas, "Biography of Anton Boisen," 1.

Despite this profound challenge to a dominant academic approach, the ANZACPE standards for accreditation as a supervisor require, among other things, four 3,000-word written papers. This requirement, as well as the dominant Western academic language embedded in the standards, demonstrates the influence of the dominant culture over alternate voices. It also diminishes Boisen's concern for a shift *from books to the raw material of life*. For example, traditional Australian Aboriginal people—such as the Bundjalung pastoral practitioners with whom I work—lack a formal written culture. They communicate primarily through cultural symbols, rituals, and stories, as well as operating as a listening and guiding presence within their community.

I initially came into the story of this group as an outsider, representing the dominant culture with all its privileges. I came onto *their* country (Jugon) and I was in *their* sacred space requiring respect (*Gurr*). It made sense to me and my culture—as a follower of the way of Jesus—to approach the situation with the utmost respect. To listen first and speak second.

Due to prevalent past racist attitudes, some Aboriginal people were refused entry into education as early as primary school; consequently, many Aboriginal people can neither read nor write in English or their traditional languages. In many cases, the Indigenous language has been lost. Recovering language has enabled some Aboriginal people to develop a greater sense of identity with less dependence on patronizing, non-indigenous processes; however, providing care is still embedded in storytelling and guiding. This can be observed at times to be significantly different from Western paradigms, such as listening and clarifying with the focus on the other person.

For many Aboriginal people the focus is never on the individual but on the story that is unfolding and its impact on the community. Even where the story emerges from an individual, such as domestic violence or alcohol abuse, the caring process still involves a communal focus in terms of response and solution. This often involves a strong emphasis on guiding the individual within a community rather than using a person-centered approach so common in CPE.

The ANZACPE regulations, line 19, note that the learning process allows for, "the addressing of the particular learning goals of each student/participant"[6] but provides no guidelines or standards for how those particular learning goals will be presented and assessed. On the other hand, the regulations clearly define how the written assessments are to be constructed, including the number of words to be used.

The concept of time is very much a Western construct. When working with many Aboriginal persons, time is relevant to the experience of the moment and the need of persons within the community at that moment. Lines 32 and 32 state, "A CPE Unit can be completed over a minimum of 10 weeks or a maximum of 44 weeks."[7] Such time delineations have existed within the CPE framework for many decades.

Interestingly, while many CPE programs demand academic excellence and rationales for what is done and why it is done, that discipline has never been applied to the requirements of time. Why does four hundred hours constitute one unit of CPE? Why does that unit require ninety hours of group supervision and ten hours of individual supervision? Why is it that different programs require different numbers of hours for face-to-face pastoral practice? Why is the concept of face-to-face the norm for pastoral practice when for some cultures individual practice is less the norm than is communal interaction?

A more common practice in some Aboriginal communities would be for the pastoral person to be interacting with a family or a man with a group of men or a woman with a group of women. Sometimes it may be a mix of both. While it is not uncommon for there to be one-on-one conversations, those conversations are also linked to communal living, including the obligations within the community.

---

6. *ANZACPE Standards*, 1.
7. *ANZACPE Standards*, 1.

Why is a CPE group required to have a minimum of three to four persons or a maximum of six? Once again, there is no rationale provided for these arbitrary numbers. In many Aboriginal communities the groups would be much larger, along with a fair degree of creative movement in and out of the group for people to come and go. There may well be a core learning group, but inevitably some cultural uncle or cousin will come along to see what is happening and join in. In a Western-oriented group that would be seen as a boundary violation. In an Aboriginal group it is seen as normal. Insisting on defining that as a boundary violation would be offensive to some Aboriginal groups depending on their situation and their relationship with the white community.

Critical for supervision within Polynesian cultures (Tonga, Aotearoa New Zealand, Samoa, Niue, Cook Islands, Tahiti, and Marquesas) are issues of hierarchy, obedience, land, family, and spirituality. Family is of the utmost importance and is closest to what non-Polynesians would call a large, extended family. Polynesians also connect strongly to their village and geographical area in which the family belongs. It is difficult for Polynesians to separate culture or family from self. They tend to develop personalities that function in community without a strong sense of decision-making independent from community. European tradition tends to emphasize individuation.[8] Polynesian culture places the individual within cultural expectations and obligation to family.[9]

The good news is the view ANZACPE takes toward the regulations; "ANZACPE views it as a 'living document' i.e., open to continuous review and adaptation."[10] This provides room for creative dialogue and adaptation, as well as fostering mutual interaction between cultural groups. This has the potential to develop CPE processes that are not only more diverse but draw their

8. Mahler, *Selected Papers*; Markus and Kitayama, "Cultures and Selves," 426.

9. Becker, *Body, Self, and Society*; Finnegan and Orbell, *South Pacific Oral Traditions*; Morton, *Becoming Tongan*; Culbertson, *Counselling Issues*; Culbertson, "Listening Differently"; Epati, *Samoan Culture*; Ihimaera, *Growing Up Māori*; Mageo, *Theorizing Self in Samoa*; Tuilotolava, *Tongan Culture*.

10. *ANZACPE Standards*, 1.

inspiration, insights, and learning models from cultures emerging from colonial disposition.

As one Tongan theologian said to me during the setting up of the initial CPE program in Tonga, "We Tongans owned our own land, unlike other Pacific nations, so the colonial powers could not take our land, but they *colonized our minds*." Embedded in this statement is a profound feeling of dispossession and a fear of repetition of that disposition. Despite all attempts on my part to be a collegial and respectful educator, there still existed in his mind the possibility that I would be like *Palangi* (white person and foreigner) who came before me.

Being aware of this sensitivity, and thinking it the most appropriate thing to do after discussion with my Tongan colleague, I attended the first training session dressed in traditional male Tongan garb. This simple act had an immediate impact on the group. The trainees experienced my action as showing deep respect for them and a willingness to join in an expression of cultural sensitivity with them. To me it just seemed to be commonsense; however for them it indicated a deeper and more respectful process than I initially realized.

Thinking I had adequately addressed the cultural issue of me coming as a stranger, I began the program with my Tongan colleague. He works alongside me to assist both with the language and translating the pastoral practice ideas being discussed. In addition, the model I use requires the educator to begin with an acceptance of ignorance of the culture within which education is taking place, along with willingness to facilitate a respectful dialectic with the students.

Despite all these assurances of respect, the Tongan theologian referred to above chose to participate in the first day to assist with translation. I noted that his translation was significantly longer than the short phrases I was using. I enquired of my educator colleague, "He seems to be saying a whole lot more than I am saying. Can you help me understand what is going on?" My colleague laughed and said, "He is decolonizing your teaching!" Rather than being offended, I was deeply moved. Even after all the time spent together providing assurances of cultural respect, the fear of me as the *Palangi* polluting the Tongan mind was still present. Once the theologian became confident that I had heard his concerns and could be trusted he went about other tasks.

POSSIBLE EDUCATIONAL CHANGES EMERGING FROM CULTURAL CHALLENGES AND DIALOGUE

As the *living human document* is a key concept in CPE, why not begin there? Why do we begin with *our* program, *our* regulations, and then attempt to adapt culturally to the other cultural group? Why not begin with the other group and ask the question, "How is what they are asking to learn assisted by the CPE process?" Then we can ask, "What will they be able to teach us during the respectful dialogue?" This can be followed by, "How will CPE change during the dialogue?" Leading to, "What will CPE look like at the end of each dialogue?"

Rather than being the *CPE missionaries* taking the *good news* to the *uneducated*, like the missionaries of old, supervisors could become facilitators of relationships of meaning where all persons involved contribute to the education. I can almost hear the question being asked as this is read, "How will standards of excellence be maintained?" Unfortunately, that very question emerges from a notion that CPE contains the wisdom to be taken to the other rather than CPE is a process that potentially can facilitate multiple creative dialectics. If Boisen and those who followed are correct, and the wisdom we seek is primarily contained in the living human documents, then the regulations and standards must emerge from those encounters. Regulations and assessment processes unconnected to the actual practice of providing care are as useless as theological and spiritual concepts not grounded in the way people live out their faith.

We may be shocked to discover that a person without any previous CPE experience teaches us profound insights and opens up awareness of pastoral encounters never before contemplated. I well remember an Aboriginal elder, who could barely read and write, presenting his final CPE unit evaluation that explained his spirituality and pastoral practice in a series of drawings including animals, people, trees, and various other objects. I was moved to tears as he led us deeply into a world that as a *White fella* I had not touched or been touched by before.

It may well be that a shift from the dominant CPE position of *containing the knowing* to a process of *mutual discovery of knowing*—including the mystery of not knowing embedded in some other cultures—may create a CPE never before contemplated. That may require us to go boldly where no one has gone before.[11]

BIBLIOGRAPHY

Australia and New Zealand Association for Clinical Pastoral Education. *ANZACPE Standards—Foundational and Advanced CPE 2022.* https://www.anzacpe.org.au/wp-content/uploads/2022/11/2022-Standards-Foundational-Advanced-CPE.pdf.

Becker, Anne E. *Body, Self, and Society: The View from Fiji.* Philadelphia: University of Pennsylvania Press, 1995.

Clebsch, William A., and Charles R. Jaekle. *Pastoral Care in Historical Perspective.* Lanham, MD: Jason Aronson, 1994.

Culbertson, Philip, ed. *Counselling Issues in South Pacific Communities.* Auckland: Accent, 1997.

———. "Listening Differently with Maori and Polynesian Clients." *Forum: Journal of the New Zealand Association of Psychotherapists* 5 (1999) 64–82.

Epati, A'ea'u Semikueiva. *Multi-Cultural Issues in Everyday Practice: Samoan Culture.* Auckland: Auckland District Law Society, 1998.

Finnegan, Ruth Hilary, and Margaret Orbell, eds. *South Pacific Oral Traditions.* Bloomington: Indiana University Press, 1995.

Gulo, Alokasih. "Some Notes on the Idea of Living Human Document and Its Implications for Pastoral Praxis." *Eduvest—Journal of Universal Studies* 2 (2022) 140–49.

Ihimaera, Witi. *Growing Up Māori.* Auckland: Tandem, 1998.

Leas, Robert. "The Biography of Anton Theophilus Boisen." Association for Clinical Pastoral Education. https://acpe.edu/docs/default-

---

11. The original phrase "by oceans where none had ventured" was coined by the Portuguese poet Luís de Camões in his poem "The Lusiads." The phrase evolved and eventually was picked up and used as "to boldly go where no man has gone before" by Captain Kirk in the 1960s television series *Star Trek*. Staniforth, "Where No Man Has Gone Before."

source/acpe-history/the-biography-of-anton-theophilus-boisen. pdf?sfvrsn=f542507_2.
Mageo, Jeannette Marie. *Theorizing Self in Samoa: Emotions, Genders, and Sexualities*. Ann Arbor: University of Michigan, 1998.
Mahler, Margaret S. *The Selected Papers of Margaret S. Mahler*. 2 vols. New York: Jason Aronson, 1982.
Markus, Hazel Rose, and Shinobu Kitayama. "Cultures and Selves: A Cycle of Mutual Constitution." *Perspectives on Psychological Science* 5 (2010) 420–30.
Morton, Helen. *Becoming Tongan: An Ethnography of Childhood*. Honolulu: University of Hawaii Press, 1996.
Staniforth, Nick. "Where Did Star Trek's 'Where No Man Has Gone Before' Line Originate? It's Complicated." Looper, Feb. 5, 2024. https://www.looper.com/1508018/star-trek-where-no-man-has-gone-before-line-origin.
Tuilotolava, Mele. *Multicultural Issues in Everyday Practice: Tongan Culture*. Auckland: Auckland District Law Society, 1998.

6

Examining the Supervisee's Journey

A Hexagonal Model for Islamic Pastoral Care in CPE Supervision

SALIH YUCEL

WHAT IS PASTORAL SUPERVISION IN THE ISLAMIC CONTEXT?

There are various definitions of pastoral supervision. Leach and Paterson define pastoral supervision as "a relationship between two or more disciples who meet to consider the ministry of one or more of them in an intentional and disciplined way."[1] The Institute of Pastoral Supervision and Reflective Practice defines pastoral supervision as an intentional dialogue between the soul (inner motivation) and the role that reflects in the field.[2] The Uniting Church in Australia defines supervision as "a safe, confidential relationship which provides a regular opportunity to reflect on our work and

---

1. Leach and Paterson, *Pastoral Supervision*, 1.
2. Institute of Pastoral Supervision and Reflective Practice, "What Is Pastoral Supervision?"

professional relationships."³ Geoff Broughton argues, "Many of the standard working definitions reflect some aspects of what pastoral supervision means, but each lacks something essential."⁴

Broughton argues, "The term supervision continues to be problematic for the pastoral context," and questions "if supervision is pastoral."⁵ This chapter supports Broughton's view that it is aligned with Islamic spiritual care. In traditional Islam, scholars view their students as their children or friends instead of seeing themselves as masters or teachers. Being seen or showing self as a supervisor can mean being superior to the supervisee. This contradicts two important Islamic spiritual practices: modesty and humbleness. However, this chapter uses supervision because it is commonly known in pastoral care in the West.

For Ibn Sina (d. 1037), the teacher is a facilitator instead of a master or supervisor.⁶ Al-Ghazali (d. 1111) views the teacher as a role model, and "the duties of a teacher are more than those of parents."⁷ His approach to guidance and education resembles that of a parent-child relationship. This relationship is not about asking a child what to do or not do, but rather, taking a compassionate parental approach. Nursi (d. 1960) views himself and his students as servants of the community in spiritual and emotional care. He says, "We are hands working on a dominical boat that will disembark the Community of Muhammad (PBUH) at the Realm of Peace, the shore of salvation."⁸ It can be said that supervision in the Islamic context is to help supervisees and learn from them simultaneously. In the parent-child relationship context, supervision is transformed into compassion, which reflects no worldly expectation except for the betterment of the supervisee in all aspects.

In my view, Islamic clinical and pastoral supervision can be defined as "combining educational, moral, and practical aspects

3. Uniting Church in Australia, "Pastoral Supervision," 3.
4. Broughton, "Supervision," 10.
5. Broughton, "Supervision," 12.
6. Yasmansyah et al., "Analysis of Educational Thought," 152–60.
7. Al-Ghazzali, "*Ihya Ulum-id-Din*," 60.
8. Nursi, *Gleams*, 227.

in a holistic approach, aiming to provide intellectual satisfaction while equipping students with spiritual and emotional care skills." It is aimed that, through these skills, the spiritual carer can help supervisees to remove obstacles between God and individuals in their religious journeys by helping emotionally, spiritually, and psychologically. This definition is based on Ibn Sina, al-Ghazali, and Nursi's works, on which the author is an expert, and their treatments for patients and students.

After this short introduction to Islamic spiritual care, a case will be analyzed using the hexagonal model.

The hexagonal model is a new theory in clinical pastoral education. It is based on an analysis of six questions, which begin with the letter W. Historically, traditional Muslim scholars used similar methods in *hadiths* (prophetic sayings) collections for authentication. These questions are: Who said it? What was said? When was it said? Why was it said? To whom was it said? Where was it said? The hexagonal model has two aims. The first is to understand the interlocutor very well in every aspect. The second is to improve the pastoral supervisor and CPE student's pastoral care skills. In this chapter, I will examine the hexagonal model in the light of Islamic sources for providing spiritual and emotional care in CPE. I have been developing and applying this theory in my supervision for the last three years. I have observed several advantages of this theory in emotional and pastoral care. It provides a more profound insight into supervisees from a pastoral care standpoint. Nevertheless, it requires additional refinement.

Firstly, the identity of the speaker is considered. This includes their social status, psychological state, and religious background. Secondly, the timing of the statement—whether it was made during moments of shock, depression, grief, anxiety, or under normal circumstances—was examined. Thirdly, the reasons behind the statement, seeking the underlying wisdom or motivation, were explored. What exactly did the speaker convey? Investigating the content accurately is crucial. Additionally, I analyze the intended audience—whom the speaker addressed. Lastly, I take into account the context in which the statement was made. This chapter delves into applying the hexagonal model in Hanna's case.

CASE STUDY: HANNA

1. Who Is Hanna?

Hanna (pseudonym) is a student at my university who is taking a CPE course. She is from a family with a Middle Eastern background and is Caucasian in appearance. Hanna was born in Australia and is culturally Australian but, by faith, a practicing Muslim. She took two of my university subjects via Zoom in the last two sessions due to COVID-19. However, she could not complete one of her assessments due to her father's serious heart illness. She enrolled upon hearing about the CPE course in Sydney, of which I am the supervisor. We could not ever meet face-to-face due to COVID-19 travel restrictions. She is in her late thirties, married, and a mother of three children. To date, I have had eight online supervision sessions with her. Hanna is empathetic and keen to help others. She has an extroverted character and finds energy in interactions with others. While facing the challenges, she becomes a bit anxious and emotional. To a certain extent, she is a perfectionist. She is talkative but also a good listener.

2. What Did Hanna Say About Her Case?

I could gather Hanna's background information based on group and individual supervision. Her father was the president of a mosque and was very active in the community. In mid-May 2021, he had a complicated heart problem and was hospitalized after a heart attack. The surgeon told him that he would have a 30 percent chance of survival if he had heart surgery. Otherwise, he could die at any time due to the severity of the heart problem. It was a frightening day for Hanna and her family. However, Hanna wanted to be strong and dissimulate her fear because this was an expectation of her father. It seemed that she was connected to her father more than her mother.

Her father took the risk and had the surgery. I was in contact with Hanna via email and tried to provide emotional and spiritual support at this difficult time. I helped her in applying for special consideration to complete her assessments later in Islamic Studies at Charles Sturt University. I prayed *Salatul Hajaat* (the Prayer of Need), which is recommended to be performed in Islam at such a difficult time and let her know. She wrote, "Please keep my father Ali [pseudonym] in your *dua* [prayer]." Initially, the surgery was successful. We exchanged two more emails. Each time, she was happy that the surgery went well.

3. When Did Hanna Say This?

The dialogue took place while her father was in the intensive care unit; Hanna tried to help a female family member of another patient in the same ward. She felt that both could support each other while experiencing a similar challenge. Initially, Hanna was hesitant because wearing a hijab could be an obstacle to a warm welcome by the patient's family member. However, she introduced herself to Paula and she warmly welcomed her. In her theological reflection, Hanna indicated that although they had different religions, both agreed that God is in control of everything. Both found prayer helpful. Later Hanna had a conversation with Paula's brother. Hanna said, "We both felt the need to support each other." One of her peers in CPE class asked what Hanna felt after the conversation and helping Paula's brother. She replied, "Satisfaction." She was so happy that Paula's brother recovered and was discharged later. Hanna could not see Paula again. These few conversations left a permanent mark on her soul. During the individual supervision, she indicated that providing emotional support to Paula and her brother resulted in satisfaction. She experienced how important it is to help others, particularly at challenging times.

Contemporary Muslim scholar Nursi states, "Know, O friend, who does not know the pleasure and happiness in labour and giving service, that out of His perfect Mercy, God the Ultimate Truth has included part of the reward for service in serving, and part of the reward for action in acting."[9] Hanna found satisfaction in helping others. Her father, through his exemplary life, injected helping others into Hanna's character.

While listening to Hanna during the individual supervision, thirteenth-century mystic Yunus Emre's (d. 1320) poem came to my mind, and I mentioned it to her. He wrote,

> We love the created,
> For the Creator's sake.[10]

Talat Halman argues that Yunus Emre "provided spiritual guidance and aesthetic enjoyment."[11] This enjoyment is spiritual. It is the satisfaction of the emotions that are reflected in Hanna's spiritual life.

A few days later, Hanna's father's health condition deteriorated. The next day, she visited and spent almost a whole day with him. She recited the chapter of Yaseen from the Qur'an upon my recommendation which is a tradition in Islam. She said, "My father was very happy with my recitation." She did not forget that moment of his happiness, which would have later helped her in her grief journey.

4. Why Did Hanna Say This?

About a week later, she wrote to me, "It is with great heartache that I inform you that I lost my best friend in the world. My father has returned to his Creator."

I sent her my condolence message indicating, "May Allah rest him in peace. I have never met him, but I feel a connection with your father. I will recite the chapter of Yaseen from the Qur'an daily [this is a tradition] for his soul. Do you have any close relatives who could help you?" I also asked her if there was anything

---

9. Nursi, *Gleams*, 171.
10. Halman, "Poetry of Yunus Emre," 233.
11. Halman, "Poetry of Yunus Emre," 234.

that I could do to help her. She responded to my email, "I am staying with my mum right now as she is not doing well. We have had *Alhamdulillah* [thanks to God] an overwhelming number of visitors" who provide help.

Later, I sent two pages from a scholarly work by Nursi on the theology of death from an Islamic perspective.[12] About a week after her father's death, I was able to organize a meeting with her via Zoom. After a short prayer for her father, I wanted to hear more about her father because she wrote that her father was also her best friend. It was the most challenging day in her life. She preferred to turn off the camera. So I did it as well. That helped me to take more notes from the conversation.

5. What Did Hanna Say to Me?

The conversation took about forty minutes. I missed a few sentences due to a poor internet connection, but she responded to all questions. Below is a part of my dialogue with Hanna.

> S1: How do you feel, Sister Hanna? (Calling someone *sister* or *brother* means spiritually you are close, like a biological sibling, in Islamic culture.)
>
> H1: Initially, it was very hard for me to accept, and I was shocked and in denial. But *Alhamdulillah* I am starting to learn that grief is a journey, that there are good moments, that there are sad moments, and that everything is from Allah.
>
> S2: I have been to the mosque where your father was president a few times, but I have never met him. Can you tell me more about your father?
>
> H2: My father was looked after by an Australian family when he emigrated as a young man from [a Middle

---

12. Nursi views death as a release from life's duties, a change of existence, and an invitation to eternal life. For humans, death is a transition to an everlasting life in the Intermediate Realm. There are four aspects of death considered bounties: freedom from life's burdens, escape from worldly limitations, relief from old age, and a merciful rest akin to sleep. See *Letters*, 5–6.

Eastern country] in 1974. Because of his English skills, he helped refugees from Arab countries and new, voluntary immigrants for decades. (I missed a part of what was said due to the poor internet connection. However, I did not want to interrupt her conversation.) One important lesson that I have learned is that my father was the backbone of our family. Once that is broken, nothing can repair it. But in saying that, I do not have despair in Allah's *hukum* [decision] for Allah always knows best.

The conversation continued. I learned that her father helped refugees and new arrivals find jobs, fill out job applications, rent houses, and interpret for them on health-related issues. He was a liaison officer between the police and the Arab community, local schools, and parents in his suburb. He initially performed Friday prayer in a local church because there was no mosque in the area. Later, the town provided a space for Friday prayer in the town hall. He established a mosque with some other community members, which took a few years. He was elected to lead the community as the president of the mosque. Due to his language skills and altruism, the community kept him in the administration position until he died. I asked Hanna,

> S3: What helped you at this difficult time?
>
> H3: My faith and community. We received great support from the community. Many visited us and offered their condolences. Someone from our community has a restaurant. For ten days, we did not cook because we received meals from that restaurant for free. (Providing food for a deceased family for seven days is a prophetic tradition in Islam.) One of my close friend's brothers passed away two years ago. She would often repeat *inna lillahi wa inna ilayhi raji'un* (Those who, when a disaster befalls them, say, "Surely we belong to God (as His creatures and servants), and surely to Him we are bound to return (and they act accordingly))." [Qur'an 2:156][13]

---

13. Unal, *Qur'an with Annotated Interpretation*, 121.

Hanna recited the same verse a lot and found that it was helpful. She said, "That was a great lesson that I learned from my friend. Initially, it was hard to accept my father's death, but I am not in denial now, and, in fact, I feel fully that the death is true."

> S4: How are you coping after the death of your lovely father?
>
> H4: Still in grief. What I experienced is that now I can understand what the loss is for a family because I am the eldest among my five siblings. My father taught me and expected me to be strong during difficult times. Upon hearing of the death of my father, I tried not to cry in the presence of my family. However, when I was alone at home, I cried for hours. The tears helped and gave me some comfort in my grief journey.

Hanna concealed her fear and grief in front of her family. Her father had taught her to serve as a role model for her siblings during challenging moments. She believed that failing to dissimulate would be disobedience to her father, and she found that this approach was effective. I was not able to tell her that this was contradictory to the prophetic tradition because the Prophet cried in the presence of his companions when his children died.[14] Hanna inherited a religionized culture from her father. I knew it was contradicting the prophetic tradition. However, I did not know how to answer at that time, or maybe could not respond due to her grief.

Grief became a treasure for Hanna's spiritual journey. She felt that it brought her closer to God. Commenting on the Qur'anic

14. Narrated Anas ibn Malik:

> We went with Allah's Messenger (ﷺ) (p.b.u.h) to the blacksmith Abu Saif, and he was the husband of the wet-nurse of Ibrahim (the son of the Prophet). Allah's Messenger (ﷺ) took Ibrahim and kissed him and smelled him and later we entered Abu Saif's house and at that time Ibrahim was in his last breaths, and the eyes of Allah's Messenger (ﷺ) (p.b.u.h) started shedding tears. `Abdur Rahman bin `Auf said, "O Allah's Apostle, even you are weeping!" He said, "O Ibn `Auf, this is mercy." Then he wept more and said, "The eyes are shedding tears and the heart is grieved, and we will not say except what pleases our Lord, O Ibrahim! Indeed we are grieved by your separation. Al-Bukhari, *Sahih al-Bukhari*, 1303 (Funerals (Al-Janaa'iz)).

verse 2:155, twelfth-century mystic al-Qushayri (d. 1072) stated, "If you are not tested with Qurb (family members, close friends, neighbors, workmates), you cannot gain the Qurb (nearness to God) spiritual station."[15]

When Hanna was talking, I learned that two happy moments left a permanent mark which helped her in coping with grief. First, a week before her father got sick, she purchased a jacket for him as an Eid gift online. While he opened the gift parcel, she recorded it on her mobile phone. In the recording, there were jokes and laughter. Hanna asked her father, "Dad, what gift are you going to purchase for me for my graduation in early December?" He responded, "Apple pie." Everyone in the room laughed. He knew that Hanna loved apple pie. She watches this recording from time to time with tears.

The second is that she spent most of her day with her dad a day before he passed away and her recitation of the Qur'an made him happy. She added, "I wish we could have had a Muslim chaplain's visit before my dad passed away." She thinks not having a Muslim chaplain at that difficult time becomes a source of motivation and encouragement for her in a CPE course. She thought about those who had the same or similar situation. I observed that Hanna's journey for chaplaincy is not just about getting a certificate but that she feels morally obliged to help such people during the crisis. She is so keen to continue her father's legacy through chaplaincy work.

The conversation continued for another twenty minutes. I found that she was so keen to continue her father's legacy. However, it seems to me that she was not clear about the priorities of this journey and how to do it. She indicated that her father was the backbone of the family. Hanna said, "Once that is broken, nothing can repair it." Hanna is looking for an answer to determine if there is any way to repair it. She thinks that doing volunteer community work will be helpful in her grief journey. Each day, each hour, a human is a different person psychologically, biologically, and

---

15. Al-Qushayri, *Lataif al-Isharat*, verse 155.

spiritually. For a chaplain or psychologist to understand a human is a life journey.

6. Where Did Hanna Say This?

How Hanna coped with grief in the presence of her siblings and mother was different than when she was alone. She did not want to appear weak and dissimulated her grief and sadness in the presence of family members. She inherited this culture from her father. She thought not applying this culture could be disrespectful to her father. However, Hanna did not hesitate to disclose when she was alone and during individual supervision. What I learned from Hanna was that macho culture, a social construction of masculinity, is not only part of the Turkic world but also Arab culture.

ANALYSIS

By applying the hexagonal model, I could obtain detailed background information and contextualize it in supervision. Knowing more about Hanna's background helped me understand the supervisee's spirituality and cultural expectations. I observed that she was devoted to her spiritual life. This triggered me to discuss grief with her not from a secular perspective but from a spiritual perspective, which led to comfort. She indicated how the statement below comforted her after we discussed it on Zoom.

Mawlana Jalal Din Rumi, a great thirteenth-century mystic, says, "Grief can be the garden of compassion. If you keep your heart open through everything, your pain can become your greatest ally in your life's search for love and wisdom."[16] In addition, he says, "Goodbyes are only for those who love with their eyes. Because for those who love with heart and soul, there is no such thing as separation."[17] The concept of death is highly discussed by Muslim scholars. In theology, death is considered "a discharge

---

16. Rumi, "Grief."
17. Rumi, "Goodbyes."

from the duties of life; it is a rest, a change of residence, a change of existence; it is an invitation to eternal life, a beginning, the introduction to immortal life. It is reuniting with loved ones who passed away."[18]

Therefore, when a Muslim dies, exaggerated expressions of loss and grief are unacceptable. Wailing and other emotionally charged expressions are not approved.[19] However, naturally as humans, we are scared of death and dislike it. Hanna's denial of the death of her beloved father has room in Islamic theology. When the prophet Muhammad passed away, some companions, such as Umar (who later became caliph), were in denial of his death. Although Hanna knew the concept of death in theology, she was confused in the first stage. When a human is in a state of shock, his or her wrong actions are forgivable. Because in such a state of shock, the smart brain is deactivated and the survival brain is activated. A human is like a half-mad person. Hanna preferred a cultural approach to a religious one in macho culture. She wanted to move on, which she later explained in one of her pastoral encounter reviews.

The loss of the father motivated her to become a chaplain in a nursing home after the CPE course. Her father's altruism left a permanent mark on Hanna. She said, "Based on the prophetic tradition, the deceased parents are happy when their children do the good things."[20] She believes that her father's soul will be happy if she does chaplaincy work.

During online supervision with Hanna, I could not convey most of the nonverbal components of my body language. Sometimes, technical difficulties or weak internet connectivity negatively impacted the quality of the tone of voice. However, the hexagonal model in CPE supervision has helped to provide emotional and spiritual support.

---

18. Nursi, *Letters*, 5–6.
19. Suhail et al., "Continuing Bonds," 24.
20. An-Nawawi, *Riyad as-Salihin* (quoting Imam Muslim's *Sahih Muslim*).

CONCLUSION

The hexagonal model in pastoral supervision provides a deeper understanding of the supervisee's emotions and spiritual, social, and psychological status. It identifies the core principles of individual pastoral identity. The hexagonal model is a methodology for comprehending the wisdom behind the supervisee's words and actions. This helps the supervisor to conceptualize available information in a pastoral care context. It also assists supervisees in clearing the pathway to continue their journey in CPE. The disadvantage of the hexagonal model is that it is difficult to apply before establishing trust. Asking too many questions before trust has been established can be perceived as an intrusion into someone's private life. In Hanna's case, I had already built good trust while teaching her for almost two years before applying the hexagonal model. The relationship between Hanna and me was like that between a spiritual brother and sister. As a result, the hexagonal model worked in this case. Thus, building very good trust before applying this model in pastoral supervision is necessary.

BIBLIOGRAPHY

Broughton, Geoff. "What Is 'Pastoral' About Supervision? A Christological Proposal." *St. Mark's Review* 254 (Dec. 2020) 9–22. https://researchoutput.csu.edu.au/en/publications/what-is-pastoral-about-supervision-a-christological-proposal.

Bukhari, Muhammad al-. *Sahih al-Bukhari*. "Funerals (Al-Janaa'iz)" Translated by M. Muhsin Khan. https://sunnah.com/bukhari:1303.

Ghazzali, Abu Hamid al-. "Revival of Religious Learnings: Imam Ghazzali's *Ihya Ulum-id-Din*." Translated by Fazl-ul-Karim. June 18, 2007. https://ghazali.org/ihya/english/ihya-vol1.htm.

Halman, Talât Sait. "Turkish Humanism and the Poetry of Yunus Emre." *Tarih Arastirmalari Dergisi* 10 (1968) 231–40. https://dergipark.org.tr/tr/download/article-file/783236.

Institute of Pastoral Supervision and Reflective Practice. "What Is Pastoral Supervision?" https://ipsrp.org.uk.

Leach, Jane, and Michael Paterson. *Pastoral Supervision: A Handbook*. 2nd ed. London: SCM, 2015.

Nawawi, Yahya ibn Sharaf an-. *Riyad as-Salihin*. https://sunnah.com/riyadussalihin:1383.

Nursi, Said Bediuzzaman. *The Gleams: Reflections on Qur'anic Wisdom and Spirituality*. The Risale-i Nur Collection. Translated by Huseyin Akarsu. Somerset, NJ: Tughra, 2008.

———. *The Letters: Epistles on Islamic Thought, Belief, and Life*. The Risale-i Nur Collection. Translated by Huseyin Akarsu. Somerset, NJ: Tughra, 2007.

Qushayri, al-. *Lataif al-Isharat*. https://www.altafsir.com/Tafasir.asp?tMadhNo=3&tTafsirNo=31&tSoraNo=2&tAyahNo=155&tDisplay=yes&UserProfile=0&LanguageId=1.

Rumi. "Goodbyes are only for those who love with their eyes. Because for those who love with heart and soul there is no such thing as separation." Goodreads. https://www.goodreads.com/quotes/662262-goodbyes-are-only-for-those-who-love-with-their-eyes.

———. "Grief can be the garden of compassion. If you keep your heart open through everything, your pain can become your greatest ally in your life's search for love." Goodreads. https://www.goodreads.com/quotes/7085354-grief-can-be-the-garden-of-compassion-if-you-keep.

Suhail, Kausar, et al. "Continuing Bonds in Bereaved Pakistani Muslims: Effects of Culture and Religion." *Death Studies* 35 (2011) 22–41. https://doi.org/10.1080/07481181003765592.

Unal, Ali. *The Qur'an with Annotated Interpretation in Modern English*. Somerset, NJ: Tughra, 2007.

Uniting Church in Australia Ministerial Education Commission. "Pastoral Supervision: Introducing a Process of Reflection on Ministry Experience." Sept. 2001. https://www.hunter.uca.org.au/wp-content/uploads/2022/01/mecpastoralsupervision.pdf.

Yasmansyah, et al. "The Analysis of Educational Thought According To Ibn Sina and Its Relevance in Islamic Education in the Modern Era." *International Journal of Humanities Education and Social Sciences* 1 (2021) 152–60.

7

Diversity in Clinical Pastoral Education

A Uniting Force

KRSNANGI MULDER

OPENING THE VISION

In a world full of quarrel and hypocrisy, and increasing day by day with division, wars and pestilence,[1] acknowledging our individual and collective life journeys among this can be a uniting force as we connect via our common human experiences. There are the miseries we each have to navigate, whether practicing spirituality or not, those miseries created by one's own mind and body, from actions of others around us and the intense power of natural disasters—extreme weather events, earthquakes, mud slides, floods, and fires.[2] Compassionate listening with empathy is much needed to mitigate and give voice to the sufferings during the course of one's life that can be isolating and devastating to the human spirit. How do we reach out beyond the temporary material identity

---

1. Bhaktivedanta Swami Prabhupada, *Srimad Bhagavatam*, 5.12.7.
2. Bhaktivedanta Swami Prabhupada, *Srimad Bhagavatam*, 1.1.2.

designations of race, culture, and even religion[3] to open this emotional and spiritual care of clinical pastoral education to everyone? Traumatic events and the grief of losses are shown to change even the biology of the function of the brain and the body,[4] affecting the way one engages in the world and one's mental and physical well-being.

Life is full of questions; we could make an estimate that there are billions upon billions posed each day. Do we ever stop to ponder how many of those tap into connecting with our ultimate concerns and are for our greatest good and that of fellow human beings? Questions pertaining to our eternal existence and identity at the same time acknowledge the temporary life journey we are all faced with: exploring our hopes, dreams, life reversals, grief, and longings.[5] How much time do we dedicate to cultivating a soft humble heart eager to be an embodiment of love and compassion in action,[6] to build upon creating an ethos in the global community of unity in diversity? Globalization has brought with it lots of changes including the movement of people to make other nations their homes by choice or for survival. This brings with it religious and spiritual diversity within community and the CPE field of activity. Diversity among the supervisors, students, and the people who receive care in a vast array of settings: hospitals, mental health facilities, aged and palliative care facilities, and correctional centers. There is a need to create opportunities for open dialogue, to have appreciation of differences, and to work collaboratively within a common compassionate cause.[7]

3. Bhaktivedanta Swami Prabhupada, *Srimad Bhagavatam*, 11.3.39.
4. Apigian, "Biology of Trauma."
5. Bhaktivedanta Swami Prabhupada, *Perfect Questions Perfect Answers*.
6. Bhaktivedanta Swami Prabhupada, *Bhagavad Gita*, 18.42.
7. Doherty, "Christian-Vaishnava Dialogue."

LENSES OF UNDERSTANDING

"Vaisnavism is sometimes known as Sanatana dharma or the eternal function of the soul, referred to also as bhakti yoga or the devotional path through which one can link with the supreme."[8] In Vaisnavism, there is the understanding of an identity that is eternal, in which all living entities are known to have an eternal function or occupation as a spirit soul.

Sanantana dharma is a principle lens in which Gaudiya Vaisnavas view and relate with the world, connecting through the understanding of us all having a core spiritual identity that is beyond our individual, current race, culture, body, and religious identity. Therefore it can be applied as a model of care that is uniting in nature, viewing the commonality of all living entities in their eternal nature as well as in the threads of life experiences that weave and highlight numerous forms of intersectionality.[9] Separateness, in a sense, is the misconception of who we are and our forgetfulness of our interconnectedness within the whole of creation, as we become enmeshed in the temporary dualities of material existence—happiness and distress, heat and cold, pain and pleasure[10]—overlooking the concepts of eternality and the permanent, ever-expanding eternal realms and relationships. This is a means to holding the highest vision for another, to be aware of their potential and not see their conditioned state as an impediment, that all have the potential to learn, grow, and transform; to respect the pace and freewill choices of the individual; to journey alongside of them with patience, discernment, kindness, and tolerance. To be grounded in the present and informed by ancient wisdom texts alongside of professional educational principles and ethics is key for sustained, effective pastoral ministry. To give equal attention to both is necessary as is the importance of being alert to not getting trapped in the polarities of focusing on either aspect of these core parts of CPE. Spirituality distinguishes this specialized area of

---

8. Rosen, *Vaisnavism*, i.
9. Ramsay, "Resisting Asymmetries of Power."
10. Bhaktivedanta Swami Prabhupada, *Bhagavad Gita*, 2.45.

education and care from other sectors and health care modalities. A valuable and much needed part of health care[11] and a means to tending to the emotional and spiritual needs enabling movement toward holistic wellness for the welfare of all, it is at times not recognized nor clearly understood.

Sanatana dharma is an eternal phenomenon in which the human being is able to realize their full potential even in the hard struggle for existence. Everyone is essentially struggling in this period on the planet, which is very troublesome.[12] The symptoms of the conditioned state are that the living entity is prone to making mistakes, has imperfect senses, has the propensity to cheat and be cheated, and can come under illusion.[13] Knowing this helps to develop deeper levels of compassion and adaptations in educational delivery, knowing that we all have our own challenges to deal with and that, when alone, we can easily break. To have a supportive pastoral companion on the journey can strengthen our resolve, build resilience, foster safe connections, help us feel valued, and provide hope in life.

The holding of space for another to share their heart in confidence is an art—an art that requires the ongoing development of virtuous qualities, diligence, and the keeping of confidentiality. The great saint Srila Rupa Gosvami describes the revealing of the heart-mind as a spiritual, loving exchange, along with inquiring confidentially, which builds cohesiveness and greater love in community.[14] Sanantana dharma is based on universal truths and values and enables one to embrace the mood of being a humble, meek, and bold servant of the servant.[15] Approaching CPE supervision in this way opens up learning not just for the student from the supervisor and peers but for the supervisor to also learn from the students. Care givers also learn from the care receivers, learning from the living human document, a concept in relational

11. Jones, "Enhancing Pastoral Care," 35.
12. Vedavyasapriya Swami, "BG4."
13. ISKCON Desire Tree, "Four Defects."
14. Bhaktivedanta Swami Prabhupada, *Nectar of Devotion*.
15. ISKCON Educational Services, "Dharma."

dynamics first proposed by the identified founder of CPE, Anton Boisen.[16] Significantly, Boisen's own lived experience with mental health challenges was the catalyst in the formation of the first stages of the development of CPE. We owe a lot to him for his courage in standing up for those struggling with their mental health, often neglected, isolated, and ostracized, and compounded by depression and anxiety.

Pastoral/spiritual care touches lives and hearts in all areas of life. The CPE program's action-reflection model of education is empowering and transformative in personal, professional, and spiritual growth, uniting people from various faiths and spiritualities in a common purpose of tending to emotional and spiritual care of others and each other while embodying love and compassion.

Self-care is part of the ethos of this ministry and a very important one for the safety and care of the care receiver and the care giver. Without self-care and engaging in pastoral care in a balanced way the pastoral practitioner/chaplain can go into burnout, compassion fatigue, and even experience a trauma freeze-like state. Vicarious trauma can be a real issue for chaplains who work for emergency services or the military; ongoing supervision and self-care for them is crucial for remaining effective and ethical in pastoral care.[17]

This solidifies the case for an increased need to also view situations through a trauma lens in order to foster empathy and provide sensitive care. The reality is that events and circumstances in recent years have impacted people in such a way that they have been left with high stress from being traumatized, and are even unaware that they are living in a trauma-induced freeze state. There is discord in society, climate disruptions, health challenges of a worldwide virus pandemic, economic challenges, and the decline in honest and truthful dealings. This all has an impact on one's emotional, mental, and physical well-being. Living with uncertainty can keep one on edge, drained of energy, and longing for stability and rest. Distinguishing reality from illusion is

16. Asquith, "Anton T. Boisen"; Gulo, "Pastoral Praxis."
17. Levy, "Deployment Stressors."

necessary. To bear witness to the pain and suffering of others requires an awareness of trauma's impact including how it can lead to emotional numbness and influence an individual's coping strategies and behaviors as well as their ability to form connections. This is where self-reflection and self-regulation meet in pastoral care—namely, control of one's mind and senses.[18] McClintock, in *Trauma-Informed Pastoral Care*, states the need for both of these in order to extend care to others and reduce secondary trauma,[19] and suggests culturally sensitive models for healing from overwhelming experiences,[20] as clergy, over a lifetime in ministry, accumulate multiple traumatic wounds that they need to regularly heal.[21] She further highlights that it is helpful for clergy to learn to recognize symptoms of trauma[22] and commit to heal individual, community, and generational trauma with care and cultural sensitivity.[23]

AS IT IS

Suffering and beauty coexist in the magnificence of the awe of the golden rising sun shimmering light on a quiet river at dawn, announcing a new, fresh day of hope, and in contrast with the sorrow and helplessness in witnessing the perils of community members left without a home and living rough on the streets of the central business district of Sydney. As the winter sun sets on the cold asphalt and concrete hardness, while people dash by in suits and heels, an old weary blanket of darkness shrouds the spirits of the destitute, forgotten, wandering, and the yearning. Material happiness can be said to be the gap between pain and suffering, which raises the question of how to grapple with the dualities of material life: wealth and poverty, connections and isolation, love

---

18. McClintock, *Trauma-Informed Pastoral Care*, 15–17.
19. McClintock, *Trauma-Informed Pastoral Care*, 109–12.
20. McClintock, *Trauma-Informed Pastoral Care*, 60.
21. McClintock, *Trauma-Informed Pastoral Care*, 50–52.
22. McClintock, *Trauma-Informed Pastoral Care*, 16.
23. McClintock, *Trauma-Informed Pastoral Care*, 124.

and hatred, empathy and apathy. To move beyond indifference to actively cultivate concern for others, to became sober, forbearing and tolerant, loving and kind, a well-wishing friend on the journey of life. Happiness and distress are like the appearance of the winter and summer seasons; they arise out of sense perception and it is helpful to learn to tolerate them without being disturbed.[24] Being equipoised in calamity and joy takes determination and grit. It does not just come about by chance; spiritual practice is the bricks and mortar of the balancing of these forces. It is the capacity to be present to the inner tensions, acknowledging and tending to the parts of the self-meeting circumstances, people, and words that evoke rivers of thoughts connected to the wounds carried within, to disappointments, and to fragility. Brené Brown asks, "*Is* there a line in the wilderness between what behavior is tolerable and what isn't? . . . Is there a line that shouldn't be crossed?" The answer was yes, and her group participants who put true belonging into practice openly discussed their boundaries. That confirmed her earlier research that the clearer and more respected the boundaries, the higher the level of empathy and compassion for others; interestingly, the fewer clear boundaries, the less openness.[25] Being discerning and equipoised, and at the same time with healthy boundaries in place, is essential. Pastoral care is not a solo endeavor. While it requires personal commitment, responsibility to learn, grow, and transform and collaboration and reflection with colleagues is needed for accountability, stability, enhancing capacity, increasing knowledge, receiving and offering feedback, and maintaining alignment with professional standards. Depending upon one's belief and approach to their spirituality there is an awareness of the influence of Divine presence, a somewhat hidden yet perceived force of uniting love, touching and moving hearts in response to an individual's personal relationship with the Divine, experience of spiritual energy, connection with a divine person, or awareness of God within the heart. His energy within every atom, present in every moment, interaction, reflection, and

---

24. Bhaktivedanta Swami Prabhupada, *Bhagavad Gita*, 2.14.
25. Brown, "Dehumanizing Always Starts with Language."

contemplation offers an empowering yet not overriding force of benevolence, cradling the spirit, opening pathways for renewal, hope, and conscious, well-wishing action.

ENCOUNTERS WITH QUIVERING HEARTS

Entering the sacred ground of spiritual care with respect, upholding the dignity of another, and striving to abate the influence of our own biases, cultural conditioning, and beliefs, along with an awareness of triggers, projections, and transference, calls for being a nonintrusive, noncontrolling presence. It involves honoring the choices of the other and holding unconditional positive regard for those with whom we journey. This is the ministry of presence: caring for the heart, the spirit soul—and these are the stories of Irene and Mateo. (Names and some details have been changed to respect privacy.)

Irene

> I opened the front wooden door to start the day and was met with a camellia bush in full bloom of soft pink flowers, being touched by the rays of the morning sun. I stopped to take in the moment; my thoughts surprisingly drifted to a care receiver, Irene, a tenacious, creative, kindhearted woman. She loved her garden in which she planted flowering shrubs including mauve azaleas and pink, white, and red camellias. She looked at the world through the eyes of a landscape artist, noticing the puffy gray and white clouds up in the blue sky above, the richness of the colors of the leaves on the trees, the gnarly shapes of each tree trunk and its branches, twisting and turning, the vibrancy of the flower petals. She loved meeting people, going for long walks in nature, swimming in the sea, and advocating for those less fortunate than her in life. Her own life changed when she reached eighty years old with a diagnosis of dementia, something she had feared and dreaded. Spending time with her was

a joy; she had such a zest for life and even in the later stages of her illness remained empathic, compassionate, thoughtful, and deeply saddened about women and children experiencing domestic violence.

On one occasion I noticed her wandering alone in a corridor, stopping and turning her head left and right, and then she would turn around on the spot. She was in her nightie, barefoot, eyes glazed, hair disheveled, pale. I moved slowly toward her as to not startle her; I spoke softly and introduced myself. It took some time before she looked at me. "I am here with you," I said. She continues to look around her. She is confused, afraid, and in a state of panic, so I make sure to respect her personal space, aware of the possibility that she is not remembering who I am. I keep my voice soft, my words spoken slowly, and leaving a space for her to find the words to respond. "This . . . place doesn't look familiar to you." I posed this question more as a statement to help her not get more anxious with the pressure of answering a question. I heard her sigh and saw her shoulders drop and some of the tension in her face dissolve, "*Well*," she said as she turned toward me, "I knew I *must* be in the *right* place." She seemed relieved, and I responded, "But it was not familiar." She nodded and held my hand. We held silence for some time. Then I added, "Others are resting in their rooms." Irene replied "*Oh*, I wondered where everyone was. Oh well, I guess I better go back to my room." As we turned the corner, Irene spoke in a strong voice, "*Oh*, I know where I am now," then called herself, with a smile on her face, "silly Billy."

Her faith was in being kind and finding the goodness in others, speaking up for injustices. An intelligent woman who could once speak six languages, she fiercely guarded her autonomy and agency. Now she cannot always remember where she is, how to dress herself. She is frail and vulnerable.

Mateo

Emigrating from Europe in his twenties, now in his sixties, and crippled with the pain of arthritis and restricted movement, he lived alone. He had a fall, was hospitalized, told that he could not return to his home as it would be unsafe for him, and he was waiting for a room in an aged care facility. He struggled with the uncertainty and the prospect of permanently entering aged care. "What is life like this?" he remarked, and threw his arms and hands in the air with disappointment and frustration. "I am still young; I want to go back to my home. I like it there, but my children said no, and I don't know what has happened to all my stuff." He distracted himself from his suffering and losses with humor, cheekiness, and even singing a song or two in his native tongue. In a later interaction with Mateo his jolly face mask dropped and his vulnerability appeared. I remained silent and waited for his words; he looked troubled and started with a description of his childhood living in a small mountain village. Then the muscles in his face tightened, his voice croaky and broken, his eyes moistened. "My father,"—he shook his head slowly, his lips pursed, body braced—"my father, he drank heavily, he was violent with me and my mother." He seemed unsure of whether to continue sharing. I inquired, "Have you spoken this before to anyone?" He looked me in the eyes. "No, I am so disappointed and ashamed." He went on, "You know, my father, he wasted all the family money. He lied and cheated and left us with absolutely nothing."

Mateo was animated and expressed what appeared to be anger he had held contained within for many years. His breathing then slowed and deepened, tensions released. *"Anyway, that's a long time ago. I came here, had a good life until I got sick."* He never spoke about it again and I respected his choice and followed his lead in the next interaction in which he shared about his faith that he took solace and hope in—his love for Mother Mary and the miracles she performed in saving his life and revealing her presence and love to him.

My Inner Landscape

Then I had an encounter with my heart quivering. With the close deaths of my mother and father I was catapulted from being their carer into an intense separation from them and the loving exchanges we shared to the storm of a grief journey—grief, one of the most challenging of feelings to be present with. I leaned in to tend to my grief, to be with it rather than ignore it and try to push it away. Many sleepless nights were experienced; cradling myself, crying was painful and my body braced with such force to stop just one tear being shed. Grief showed up in my body with chest and muscle pain in between my ribs; it was debilitating. To reach to turn on a tap to pour water into a cup instigated relentless pain for hours. I was already physically strained and depleted from the care giving, especially extending two lots of palliative care in two months. I had been mindful to maintain self-care throughout that yet the rest just wasn't sufficient. I reached out for pastoral care which became my lifeline, the thread holding me up. One loss can open us to other losses that we have not processed or mourned. One night, lying alone at 1:00 a.m. waiting for sleep, my body began to shake. I sat up, leaning over my legs, my mouth opened wide, and a primeval wailing sound flowed out from the depths of my belly and heart, piercing the silence of the early morning. It was a blessed moment as it was the expression and release of a silent, disenfranchised grief connected to a traumatic childhood event that had left me frozen in fear to speak anything about it, with the belief that I would be in danger if I let out the sound of a cry. I was bathed in gratitude for the divine support and for what the all merciful LORD had resourced me with to heal the deep black crater of wounds within me, calling for greater self-compassion, to be gentle and loving toward myself, to pastorally tend to my heart with empathy and understanding.

THE CORE OF IT

Ultimately, the core needs we all have are to love and be loved, to experience a sense of safety in connections and true belonging;

we each at some time in our life are touched by the wild edge of sorrow.[26] Community is a vital ingredient at every stage in our life: basic human needs (belonging), physical and mental well-being (security and presence), purpose (engaging in activity that benefits humankind), and joy (wonder, mindfulness, and play).[27] In essence, CPE in itself is a uniting force in fostering diversity in collaboration, building more love and trust in community, one heart at a time. It is a benevolent pathway of living one's faith/spirituality, embodying the virtues common in all faiths, meeting each other where we are in our life journeys with compassion and respect. It boils down to the choices we make, does it not? How we choose to utilize our freewill and energy. How we are present with ourselves, others, the perspectives and approaches held. We can be united through our common human experiences, through taking self-responsibility, nurturing the purification of our consciousness and the heightening of our awareness.

BIBLIOGRAPHY

Agrawal, Radha. *Belong: Find Your People, Create Community, and Live a More Connected Life*. New York: Workman, 2018.

Apigian, Aimie. "The Biology of Trauma and Its Impact on Your Health." Believe Big, June 4, 2024. YouTube video. https://www.youtube.com/watch?v=pZE3NRCYCP4.

Asquith, Glenn H., Jr. "Anton T. Boisen and the Study of 'Living Human Documents.'" *Journal of Presbyterian History* 60 (1982) 244–65.

Bhaktivedanta Swami Prabhupada, A. C. *Bhagavad Gita as It Is*. Riverstone, Australia: Bhaktivedanta Book Trust, 2014.

———. *The Nectar of Devotion*. Mumbai: Bhaktivedanta Book Trust, 1998.

———. *The Nectar of Instruction*. Mumbai: Bhaktivedanta Book Trust, 1998.

———. *Perfect Questions Perfect Answers*. Botany, Australia: Bhaktivedanta Book Trust, 1983.

———. *Srimad Bhagavatam*. 12 Cantos. Mumbai: Bhaktivedanta Book Trust, 2018.

Brown, Brené. *Braving the Wilderness: The Quest for True Belonging and the Courage to Stand Alone*. London: Penguin Random House, 2017.

---

26. Weller, *Wild Edge of Sorrow*.
27. Agrawal, *Belong*, 12.

———. "Dehumanizing Always Starts with Language." Brené Brown, May 17, 2018. https://brenebrown.com/articles/2018/05/17/dehumanizing-always-starts-with-language.

Doherty, John. "Christian-Vaishnava Dialogue in the US: An Action-Research Minor Field Study." PhD diss., Södertörn University, 2015.

Goswami, Tamal Krishna. *A Living Theology of Krishna Bhakti: Essential Teaching of A. C. Bhaktivedanta Swami Prabhupada.* Edited by Graham M. Schweig. New York: Oxford University Press, 2012.

Gulo, Alokasih. "Some Notes on the Idea of Living Human Document and Its Implications for Pastoral Praxis." *Journal of Universal Studies* 2 (2022) 140–49.

ISKCON Desire Tree. "The Four Defects of the Conditioned Soul." Nov. 16, 2016. https://iskcondesiretree.com/profiles/blogs/the-four-defects-of-the-conditioned-soul.

ISKCON Educational Services. "Dharma (Part 1): Sanatana-Dharma." https://iskconeducationalservices.org/HoH/concepts/key-concepts/sanatana-dharma/.

Jones, Angela Roberts. "Enhancing Pastoral Care and Support by Providing Opportunities for Spiritual Growth and Transformation to Crisis and Trauma Sufferers." PhD diss., Liberty University, 2020.

Lee, Sang Taek, and Alan Galt, eds. *You Visited Me: Encouraging Spiritual Practice in a Secular World.* Eugene, OR: Wipf and Stock, 2021.

Levy, Hannah C., et al. "Deployment Stressors and Outcomes Among Air Force Chaplains." *Journal of Traumatic Stress* 24 (2011) 342–46.

McClintock, Karen A. *Trauma-Informed Pastoral Care: How to Respond when Things Fall Apart.* Minneapolis: Fortress, 2022.

O'Connor, Mary-Frances. *The Grieving Brain: The Surprising Science of How We Learn from Love and Loss.* New York: Harper One, 2022.

Ramsay, Nancy J. "Resisting Asymmetries of Power: Intersectionality as a Resource for Practices of Care." *Journal of Pastoral Theology* 27 (2017) 83–97.

Richardson, Cheryl. *The Art of Extreme Self-Care: 12 Practical and Inspiring Ways to Love Yourself More.* New York: Hay House, 2019.

Rohr, Richard. *Everything Belongs: The Gift of Contemplative Prayer.* New York: Crossroad, 2023.

Rosen, Steven, ed. *Vaisnavism: Contemporary Scholars Discuss the Gaudiya Tradition.* New York: Folk Books, 1992.

Streets, Frederick. "Social Work and a Trauma-Informed Ministry and Pastoral Care: A Collaborative Agenda." *Social Work and Christianity* 42 (2015) 470–87.

Vedavyasapriya Swami. "BG4 8 24July2024 Sydney Evening." Vedavyasapriya Swami Media, Bhagavad Gita Lecture, ISKCON Sydney Temple, Aug. 9, 2024. YouTube video. https://www.youtube.com/watch?v=QHzFpiREne8.

Weller, Francis. *Wild Edge of Sorrow: Rituals of Renewal and the Sacred Work of Grief.* Berkeley, CA: North Atlantic, 2015.

8

Embracing Gender Diversity in the CPE Group Context

BARBARA HALL

INTRODUCTION

In this chapter I will demonstrate an awareness of gender diversity drawn from the experience of having a student who identifies as a nonbinary member of the LGBTQIA+ community. The student is a member of the Uniting Church in Australia. I will compare my social and professional contexts with my student's context and discuss some of the ethical considerations of supervising the student such as respectfully remembering to use their preferred pronoun and apologizing for the times I slip up and refer to them as their gender assigned at birth. I will explore the values of the educational institution and the workplace where the student conducts their pastoral practice. I will refer to Scripture passages that reference gender diversity. Lastly, I will discuss the professional demands and expectations of the accrediting body and consider the impact of faith traditions.

THE SUPERVISOR'S SOCIAL AND PROFESSIONAL CONTEXT

My social context is that I am a heterosexual woman, married for fifty-one years, with four adult children and seven grandchildren. I am a practicing Catholic, involved in parish liturgical activities, and, up until four months ago, worked for the Catholic Archdiocese in pastoral care ministry at the local hospital. I have good working relationships with the priests assigned to our parish where we have worshipped for the past thirty-five years. In the past couple of years, I have realized that I am a progressive rather than orthodox Catholic, due in part to the fact that one of our own daughters is gay. Since coming out to us twenty years ago, she is now in a long-term relationship and engaged to be married. Our youngest grandson told me matter-of-factly last year that he was bisexual, and I was able to hear this statement from him calmly, taking onboard what he said without being shocked.

My professional context is that I have received excellent professional pastoral supervision from two gay women and two heterosexual women over a period of fifteen years. This means I have not only received the gift of their professional expertise but also their compassion and love for all humankind, arising from their life experience and struggle. Their sexual orientation has not been a factor that has impacted me; in fact, they both taught me to be more open and nonjudgmental in my approach to patients and students.

In October 2021 I received an inquiry about safe pastoral training pathways for people who identify as nonbinary from a Uniting Church minister in charge of a parish. I was able to assure her that I was personally open to accepting gender diverse people into a group. I stated that while I would endeavor to keep the group space as safe as possible, I could not guarantee the personal prejudices of future participants. Soon after a nonbinary person enrolled in an introductory course I was preparing to run online from November to December 2021. There were nine participants in the group, and for the first time I was introduced to pronouns, with this participant including "they/them" after their name on the screen. Before long, a couple of other participants also included their pronouns—typing "she/her" after their names. This action felt affirming for the nonbinary person and helped me with my understanding. Throughout the course I was very mindful of using their correct pronouns. It was easy talking to the person, but I would often get tripped up (and still do at times) when talking about them. This person enrolled in the CPE 1 graduate course that ran from February until June 2023.

THE SUPERVISEE'S SOCIAL AND PROFESSIONAL CONTEXT

My supervisee, whom I will call Lesley, was aged fifty-eight. They struggled with their sexual identity most of their life. Some years ago, Lesley made the decision to formally change their name by deed poll and identify as nonbinary. Since making that choice it has made a huge difference in Lesley's life, leading to new understandings and the claim that this decision has saved their life. They have also searched for meaning in different faith groups, such as Druid, Sufi, Quaker, and Buddhist faiths. Lesley has deepened their spirituality and found God to be more relevant these days in the Christian faith. For a time Lesley wondered whether there was a place for them in ordained ministry. Following a period of discernment, they knew it was pastoral care, particularly to the LGBTQIA+ Christian community, that they felt called to rather than ordination, which would have presented difficulties.

In the CPE group they are one of four students and have fit in well with the other three, all of whom are women. I intentionally worked to model being a nonjudgmental, caring presence and ensured there was total acceptance of their gender by trying hard to remember to use their correct pronouns. If one of the students forgot I would gently remind them in private, and before long they were totally onboard. A warmth was felt within the peer group; they were very affirming of each other, and Lesley was a real gift to the group. While there was no personal judgment or criticism, the peer group was not afraid to challenge each other in their practice of offering pastoral care to patients.

In their mid-unit evaluation Lesley reported on their progress with one of their learning goals, *"To further develop the skill of offering pastoral care to gender diverse people."* Lesley writes,

> No one has mentioned gender or pronouns to me [yet] during a [hospital] visit. I do know from experience that some gender diverse people will revert to their birth gender for a hospital [admission] because they cannot deal with the conflict they think they will experience. I have had several opportunities to offer pastoral care to gender diverse people [in the community]. These have all [been] good learning experiences. Most spiritual care conversations have been with transgender women and focused on the difficulties they face with families, work, and [with the folk] at church. All the conversations with gender diverse people have given me a deeper insight into the issues and struggles these people experience.

When visiting patients at the hospital, Lesley chooses to wear a small badge that says "they/them." I was concerned that the badge would draw the patient's attention and become the focus of the pastoral visit, so during individual supervision I asked what Lesley's intention was in wearing the badge. Lesley explained, "To indicate to any patients that may be transgender or gay that, as the pastoral carer, I am an ally, someone the patient can trust to open up to if they want to, without being judged." This is an example of Lesley's sensitivity to the vulnerability and anxiety that are common experiences for members of the LGBTQIA+ community. Lesley shared that transgender women who would normally shave twice a day found being sick in hospital made that difficult and can make them feel exposed and open to ridicule.

ETHICAL CONSIDERATIONS

Living with the awareness that one is "different" can lead gender diverse people to feel lonely, isolated, anxious, and depressed.

Society judges them to be "less than." Compassion and empathy are essential ingredients when offering pastoral care to these people as they are often marginalized. According to Carroll and Shaw, "Developing empathy (the ability to experience the feelings of others as if they were our own) is crucial to being ethically alert."[1] However, Carroll and Shaw go on to say, "Where there are differences (race, culture, gender, age, sexual orientation) it can be more difficult to elicit empathy, especially if that difference is one that causes us problems."[2] Focusing on the differences leads to "dehumanizing others" and this can preclude the other from being seen as a relatable person, someone just like us in many ways except for their sexual orientation. Baron-Cohen offers a new theory of human cruelty that moves away from the term *evil* and suggests the phrase *empathy erosion*. For Baron-Cohen lack of empathy is the reason why cruelty enters our world.[3] It is crucial that in CPE groups this phenomenon is addressed and challenged. It would be unethical to ignore this predisposition if it became apparent within the student cohort.

Evidence in a recent statistical survey titled *Snapshot of Mental Health and Suicide Prevention Statistics for LGBTIQ+ People*, published on May 13, 2021, states "Although many lesbian, gay, bisexual, transgender, intersex, queer people and other sexuality and gender diverse (LGBTIQ+) people live healthy and happy lives, research has demonstrated that a disproportionate number experience poorer mental health outcomes and have higher risk of suicidal behaviors than their peers.[4] These health outcomes are directly related to experiences of stigma, prejudice, discrimination, and abuse based on being LGBTIQ+."[5]

---

1. Carroll and Shaw, *Ethical Maturity*, 153.

2. Carroll and Shaw, *Ethical Maturity*, 154.

3. Baron-Cohen, *Zero Degrees* (quoted in Carroll and Shaw, *Ethical Maturity*, 155).

4. Thirty-five percent of transgender and gender diverse people attempt suicide compared to 3.2 percent of the general population. LGBTIQ+ Health Australia, *Snapshot*, 3.

5. LGBTIQ+ Health Australia, *Snapshot*, 1.

In a recent Pastoral Encounter Review presentation to the group, Lesley described being confronted by a patient who came up close, invading their personal space by standing directly in front of their face. Lesley froze. My supervisory strategy was to encourage and remind Lesley that they had authority to be there and suggested that they could calmly and confidently ask the patient to take a step back, as they were too close. Kirby states, "Helping students learn new responses to rejection and become able to depersonalize patient and peer behavior can be an empowering and corrective healing experience."[6] This was something that Lesley has been able to put into practice, along with learning to accept affirmation and compliments from peers, patients, and their family members, and it has been life-changing for Lesley.

SOCIAL ATTITUDES AND POLICIES IN RELATION TO THE CLIENT GROUP, STUDENTS, AND SUPERVISOR

As professional educators who train and supervise pastoral/spiritual care practitioners and chaplains it is incumbent on NSWC-CPE Centre directors to ensure that supervisors working within their CPE Centres are not biased or prejudiced toward gender diverse people. By extension, this would also apply to the executive committee who have oversight of the day-to-day workings of the college and the college council. Under the *Fair Work Act 2009*, it is unlawful to discriminate against someone based on their sexual orientation, gender identity, HIV status, family responsibilities or relationship status.[7] The Fair Work Commission has instituted the *Sex Discrimination Act 1984* which "provides that a person discriminates against another person on the ground of the gender identity of a person if the discrimination occurs by reason of:

- the gender identity of the aggrieved person,

---

6. Kirby, "LGBT Students in CPE," 35.
7. *Fair Work Act 2009* (Cth) reg. 351 (Australia).

- a characteristic that applies generally to persons who have the same gender identity as the aggrieved person, or
- a characteristic that is generally imputed to persons who have the same gender identity as the aggrieved person.

This includes a person with an intersex status. The sex of a person may include the gender assigned to a post-operative transsexual."[8]

An essential component of pastoral care education is related to emotional integration and, according to Kirby, one CPE outcome is to demonstrate "clear and responsible boundaries."[9] Kirby goes on to say, "In my experience, professional boundary training is typically hetero-normative, meaning that it assumes a heterosexual audience. In general, LGBTQ people have different expectations about boundaries than heterosexual people. For example, because it was once common for LGBTQ people to lose their job if they were discovered to be 'gay,' it became an unwritten rule not to reveal someone else's sexuality without their permission. This boundary is still followed, and it is important for CPE educators to be sensitive to 'outing' students, particularly taking into consideration where they are from and where they hope to work."[10] In the public health system, in my somewhat limited experience, it no longer seems to be an issue these days for a staff member to be gay or gender diverse.

INSTITUTION'S ETHOS (VALUES)

The "CORE" values of *collaboration, openness, respect,* and *empowerment* are fundamental within the local health district where I have practiced pastoral care for thirty years. This is the working environment wherein CPE students from our CPE Centre undertake their clinical pastoral placements. Students are welcomed, included, and encouraged to engage with staff to assist their learning and understanding of the patients' experiences. Lesley is one of the

8. Fair Work Commission, "Gender Identity."
9. Kirby, "LGBT Students in CPE," 36.
10. Kirby, "LGBT Students in CPE," 37.

pastoral care volunteers who works one day a week as part of the chaplaincy and pastoral care team, and their input is respected and appreciated by staff and pastoral care colleagues alike.

The mission of the NSW College of Clinical Pastoral Education is to deliver quality education in pastoral care and supervision characterized by:

- Excellence in the development of pastoral carers
- Equipping for effective pastoral relationships
- Commitment to reflective learning
- Engagement in theological/spiritual reflection on life experience, and
- Research in and ongoing dialogue on pastoral care and supervision.[11]

The CPE Centre where I work is closely aligned with the health district and CPE College, firstly as a registered Centre of NSW-CCPE and secondly being co-located with the Chaplaincy and Pastoral Care Department within the hospital. It is a tripartite, collaborative relationship which is essential for the smooth operation of the Centre and placement of CPE students. Lesley is the first known gender diverse student to be enrolled in a CPE program with the Centre and to be included as part of the pastoral care team at the hospital.

PROFESSIONAL DEMANDS AND EXPECTATIONS OF ACCREDITING AGENCY (NSWCCPE AND SCD)

In foundational units of CPE, students are expected to achieve specific learning outcomes to pass the course and receive a certificate. In CPE 1, one such learning outcome is to "integrate their theological/spiritual beliefs with their pastoral ministry practice." This could assume that the student is associated with a particular faith tradition or spiritual group. Kirby asserts, "In the USA, an

---

11. NSWCCPE, "Delivering Quality Education."

overwhelming number of LGBTQ students come to CPE needing, to some degree or another, to reconcile their religious heritage with their LGBTQ identity. Sixteen of the nineteen residents I worked with are now affiliated with a different denomination or spiritual practice than their childhood faith group. Sometimes this transition happened because of CPE, and sometimes it happened years earlier."[12] The issue of spirituality is very relevant for today and needs to be considered more broadly as students are asked to reflect theologically and spiritually on their pastoral encounters all the way through their CPE journey.

In Australia, work is being done in the aged care sector to "provide an environment for safe, accessible and open discussion to foster an understanding of the history and experiences of older LGBTI people and how these may impact their access to aged care services."[13] The research goes on to state that their aim is to provide a "body of knowledge and frameworks to services and staff providing support to older people across the aging and aged care sector to enable them to understand experiences and needs, and work toward the development of LGBTI inclusive environments for people of diverse genders, sexualities, and sex characteristics."[14] This work will be very helpful for spiritual and pastoral carers entering the aged care sector while at the same time be confronting for some, particularly those with traditional religious views that are not accepting of gender diversity.

FAITH GROUP EXPECTATIONS

As previously mentioned, my faith tradition is Catholic, where gender diversity is not accepted as widely as in the Uniting Church, for example. In my recent theological studies I have learned enough to feel confident that my stance of embracing gender diversity in the CPE programs I conduct is a moral and ethical choice I am free to

12. Kirby, "LGBT Students in CPE," 33.
13. Rainbow Health Australia, "Rainbows Don't Fade."
14. Rainbow Health Australia, "Rainbows Don't Fade."

make, and obliged to make, according to the law. I was delighted to hear recently that Pope Francis has approved the blessing of same-sex couples, which has been touted as a major step forward in the church's ministry to the LGBTQ community. I hope and pray, for the sake of my own daughter and gender diverse people of faith, especially those who are baptized Catholic, that the Catholic Church in Australia will hear and take to heart the words of Pope Francis and welcome all people to the altar. A few months ago, I heard a verse from Scripture being quoted by a senior clinical pastoral educator that resonated with me. It was Paul's Letter to the Galatians and the words that struck me were, "There is neither male nor female, for you are all one in Christ Jesus."[15] Of course! Clearly gender does not matter to Jesus—we are all the same to him. In their essay, Lesley wrote, "One of the most affirming stories for gender diverse people in the Bible is the encounter between Phillip and the Ethiopian eunuch in Acts 8:26–40. Eunuchs during that time would have been barred from inclusion in God's community because of their sexual otherness. The eunuch's question to Phillip, 'What prevents me from becoming baptized?' shows that sexual status is not a barrier to inclusion in God's eyes." This was from Lesley's paper in Assessment 3 of the CPE unit. I have always wondered about the church's explanation of eunuchs in the Bible as they are described as neither male nor female. Were there gender diverse people in Jesus' day too? It seems so.

CONCLUSION

In this chapter I have demonstrated an awareness of gender diversity drawn from the experience of having a student who identifies as a nonbinary member of the LGBTQIA+ community. I have compared the social and professional contexts of my student and myself and discussed some of the ethical considerations of supervising them. I have explored the values of the educational institution and the workplace where the student conducts their pastoral

---

15. Galatians 3:28 RSVCE.

practice. I discussed the professional demands and expectations of the accrediting body, and considered the impact of faith traditions. I also included two references to Scripture. I used the preferred pronoun of they/them when referring to Lesley.

BIBLIOGRAPHY

Baron-Cohen, Simon. *Zero Degrees of Empathy: A New Theory of Human Cruelty*. London: Penguin, 2011.

Carroll, Michael, and Elisabeth Shaw. *Ethical Maturity in the Helping Professions: Making Difficult Life and Work Decisions*. London: Jessica Kingsley, 2012.

Fair Work Act 2009 (Cth) (Australia). https://www.legislation.gov.au/C2009A00028/latest/text.

Fair Work Commission. "Gender Identity and Sexual Orientation." https://www.fwc.gov.au/gender-identity-sexual-orientation.

Hawkins, Peter, and Aisling McMahon. *Supervision in the Helping Profession*. 5th ed. London: Open University Press, 2020.

Kirby, Michelle. "LGBT Students in CPE: Learning, Educating, Serving." *Reflective Practice: Formation and Supervision in Ministry* 39 (2019) 31–40.

Leach, Jane, and Michael Paterson. *Pastoral Supervision: A Handbook*. 2nd ed. London: SCM, 2015.

LGBTIQ+ Health Australia. *Snapshot of Mental Health and Suicide Prevention Statistics for LGBTIQ+ People*. Oct. 2021. https://assets.nationbuilder.com/lgbtihealth/pages/549/attachments/original/1648014801/24.10.21_Snapshot_of_MHSP_Statistics_for_LGBTIQ__People_-_Revised.pdf.

NSW College of Clinical Pastoral Education. "Delivering Quality Education in Pastoral Care and Supervision." https://www.nswccpe.edu.au.

Rainbow Health Australia. "Rainbows Don't Fade with Age—LGBTI Ageing and Aged Care Training." https://rainbowhealthaustralia.org.au/training-programs/silver-rainbow-training.

Rainbow Health Victoria. *Research Matters: How Many People Are LGBTIQ?* 2020. https://www.rainbowhealthvic.org.au/media/pages/research-resources/research-matters-how-many-people-are-lgbtiq/4170611962-1612761890/researchmatters-numbers-lgbtiq.pdf.

9

A Minestrone of Mental Health Ministry

ROSEMARIE SAY

THE DANCE OF LIFE[1]

"I'm going to kill you now..."

As a fledgling psychiatric nurse, I was on my own at midnight, doing the rounds of a "back ward"—an old two-story building. Upstairs, the long dark corridor had single rooms on either side. The banging from one caused me to look through the peephole in the heavy wooden door. It was Sam,[2] the gentle giant I knew so well from day duty. She wanted to go to the loo. Ignoring firm instructions I had been given not to unlock any rooms, I let her out and followed her down the corridor. She was a whimsical sight—mincing along with the open-down-the-back, short, white, cotton hospital gown flapping away from her bare backside. We

---

1. *The Dance of life*: Edvard Munch's haunting painting is a grim reminder of the vagaries and fleetingness of our existence. He was obsessed with *memento mori* (Latin for "remember you must die"). He writes "Sickness and madness and death were the black angels that stood by my cradle." Mocerino, "Edvard Munch."

2. Sam is a pseudonym. Pseudonyms have been used throughout this chapter to protect the individuals.

entered the bathroom and she disappeared into the loo. And I stood nearby waiting...

"I'm going to kill you now..." I spun around. Sam had me cornered... She towered over me, a heavy, iron mop bucket held high above her head. Horrified, I stared up at her whiskered face. My life of seventeen years flashed past me. If only I could press the rewind button!

Suddenly a bright voice came from within me, "Shall we dance?"

Where that voice came from, I'll never know. Sam, surprised as I was, stared for a couple of seconds, and then giggled. The mop bucket went down, and she outstretched her arms. She continued to giggle... and we waltzed back to the cell from which I had released her.

I gave her an almighty push at the door, and slammed it, grabbing my key with fumbling hands. As in a recurring nightmare, I struggled to lock her in, then ran terrified to the safety of the nurses' office.

"There is a time for everything... a time to die... and a time to dance..."[3]

That simple three-word response, "Shall we dance?" had saved my life. I hadn't known that Sam was a forensic patient. Before admission, she had killed on impulse. Somehow I had managed to switch her mindset. How? I don't know. Perhaps it triggered another personality? Perhaps by offering to become her dancing partner, my arms outstretched making me totally vulnerable,[4] I became a fellow human being, regardless of my nurse's stiff and starched uniform and controlling keys?

Psychiatric nursing in the early 1960s was a harsh regime that stripped the identity and dignity of the incarcerated souls, trapping many in a nightmare. The incidents of abuse and assault horrified me, and I felt helpless. We had no supervision, no debriefing, just layers of unprocessed emotions.

3. Ecclesiastes 3:1–2, 4.

4. "Staying vulnerable is a risk we have to take if we want to experience connection." Brown, *Gifts of Imperfection*, 69.

At one point in the *Call the Midwife* TV series, the midwife, feeling overwhelmed by conditions in the London slums, says, "I didn't know people lived like this." The nun replies, "But they do. And it's why we're here."[5] That's how I felt. My call into the dark places was imperative, and I stayed in the system believing I could make a difference.

And when, in loyalty to my Florence Nightingale pledge,[6] I refused to go on strike with the other nurses, I was "sent to Coventry."[7] Even my friends rejected me. Then I really related to my patients' exile from society. "The real evil in mental illness is not to be found in the conflict, but in the sense of isolation or estrangement."[8]

Those chilling words "I'm going to kill you now" haunted me for decades. They lured me back forty years later to lay the ghosts from my past to rest. In 1999, I made a phone call enquiring about the Rozelle Hospital CPE[9] program. Reverend Alan Galt invited me to join. It was a watershed moment, shaping my future.

Since then, I have been passionate about mental health ministry, and educating, supervising, and encouraging others. Like me, so many people have carried stories of fear and trauma that prevent them entering the dark places. Stigma is based on fear—fear that is fueled by melodramatic media headlines and graphic films.[10]

    5. Lowthorpe, *Call the Midwife*. *Call the Midwife* is a British period drama television series about a group of nurse midwives working in the East End of London in the late 1950s and 1960s.

    6. "I solemnly pledge myself before God . . . to practise my profession faithfully . . . With loyalty will I . . . devote myself to the welfare of those committed to my care." The *Florence Nightingale Pledge* was created in 1893 by a committee led by Lystra Gretter, but was still taken seriously in my day. Truth About Nursing, "Nightingale Pledge."

    7. "Send to Coventry" is an idiom used in England meaning to deliberately ostracize someone. Typically this is done by not talking to them, avoiding their company, and acting as if they no longer exist.

    8. Boisen, *Exploration of the Inner world*, 268.

    9. "Clinical Pastoral Education" was introduced in 1925 at Worcester State Hospital, Massachusetts, by Anton Boisen from his own experience of mental illness.

    10. A film that affected many people is *One Flew Over the Cuckoo's Nest*, a

SAY | A MINESTRONE OF MENTAL HEALTH MINISTRY

The scariest part for some of our students is walking through the hospital gates.

In the 1950s, Macquarie Hospital was the first Australian hospital to be built without walls. This was seen as revolutionary.[11] But as Jodie, who suffers with bipolar illness, said to me, "The walls are still there, but they're invisible. When I walk down the street, I can see by people's reactions that they know I'm from the hospital." These are the walls of stigma, built with the bricks of fear and ignorance.

I hope to reduce this stigma as I share the unique rewards of mental health ministry by offering a *minestrone*[12] of anecdotes and reflections, and my love for the people.

In my years as a nurse, every patient had a diagnosis. It was "us and them"—the person subservient to the label. As a pastoral care student, there was no longer this separation. I was there to accompany people on their journey,[13] rather than "to fix" them. And I learned from them!

During my first chapel service, I asked Gary (the chaplain) to lead the patients' prayers. Arthur, a traumatized war veteran and long-term patient, signaled immediately. We could not hear his prayer as there was an ambulance siren sounding in the background. Gary asked Arthur to repeat, but we still could not understand. My impatience grew, but, with his usual respect and care,

---

1975 American psychological drama film directed by Milos Forman.

11. The NSW governor, Her Excellency Marie Bashir, joined staff of Macquarie Hospital as the hospital celebrated its fiftieth anniversary on Saturday, September 12, 2009. In her speech, the governor noted that Macquarie was the first hospital for the mentally ill in NSW that was built without walls. She expressed her admiration for Governor Lachlan Macquarie, after whom the hospital is named, commenting that he showed his compassion for those with a mental illness at a time when understanding and treatment was in its infancy.

12. From Italian *minestrone*, "that which is served," from Latin *minestrare*, "to serve."

13. "Companions on the Journey" has become the theme song in Macquarie Hospital Chapel.

Gary moved down to the back row and listened closely. Turning to the congregation, he said, "Arthur would like a prayer for the person in the ambulance whose siren we can hear." Arthur nodded vigorously.

How humbling—the sound of the siren which I saw as a nuisance because it was interfering with the smooth running of *my* service was painful to Arthur who was well in touch with life's suffering. Arthur, "the living, human document,"[14] taught me about priorities and the importance of compassion.

As for the unknown person in the ambulance . . . perhaps the only person in the world offering up a prayer for him was an old man in a "lunatic asylum"[15] who owned nothing—not even a pair of teeth—but a huge heart for humanity! The outsider might see such a person as useless . . . but when someone is in crisis, what they most often ask for is prayer. That is all Arthur had to give—and he gave it. I realized that we encounter Christ as surely if not more so among "the least of these" (Matt 25:40).

> It was as if I suddenly saw the secret beauty of their hearts, the depths of their hearts where neither sin nor desire nor self-knowledge can reach, the core of their reality, the person that each one is in God's eyes.[16]

A recent poignant prayer from one of our chapel attendees was to be "born again"—but this time "normal." I reassured her, "Lily, we love you just as you are!"[17] In his reflection "Don't Change," Anthony De Mello reminds us of the godly power of unconditional love.

> I was a neurotic for years. Anxious, depressed, selfish. And everyone kept telling me to change.
> And I resented them, and agreed with them, and wanted to change, but simply couldn't, no matter how I tried.

---

14. Boisen, *Exploration of the Inner World*, 9–10. In 1925, Boisen proposed the concept of a *living human document*, a suffering person from whom we can learn.

15. In the 1960s, the hospital was still often referred to as the "Lunatic Asylum" or the "Loony Bin."

16. Merton, *Conjectures of a Guilty Bystander*, 156–58.

17. "Come as You Are" is a favorite song in Macquarie Chapel.

What hurt the most was that, like the others, my closest friend kept urging me to change. So I felt powerless and trapped. One day he said "Don't change. I love you as you are." Those words were music to my ears: "Don't change. Don't change. Don't change . . . I love you as you are." I relaxed. I came alive. And, suddenly, I changed![18]

The worst thing about mental illness must be the rejection, the aloneness. "This is the only church where I have not felt judged,"[19] said Liam sadly. Martin Buber, in dialogue with Carl Rogers, suggests that accepting persons as they are lessens their need for defensive barriers and is the strongest factor in bringing about change.[20]

The chaplains' job is to *listen*—and to take their patients *seriously*. Hugh Mackay maintains that the desire to be taken seriously is the most important human need.[21] "And those who were seen dancing were thought to be insane by those who could not hear the music."[22] We listen for the "music" behind the words. No matter how bizarre the story, the feelings are real and they need to be validated.

During a pastoral group, we showed a DVD entitled *The Life of Jesus*. Sandy was muttering, "That's my uncle," "I went to school with that one," etc. Katie erupted, "Shut up you f-ing little shit!" and screamed abuse for the next five minutes. Bob got up and put the radio on full pelt, and that was the end of *The Life of Jesus*! The next morning Katie came to him and said, "I'm sorry I was bad-tempered yesterday—here's a Christmas present for you. And I've apologized to Sandy and given her one of my best bracelets. She's happy."

---

18. De Mello, *Song of the Bird*, 77–78 (ellipsis in original).
19. Patient's feedback from Macquarie Hospital Chapel Services.
20. Kirschenbaum and Henderson, *Rogers—Dialogues*, 61.
21. Mackay, *What Makes Us Tick?*, x.
22. A popular quote often attributed to Friedrich Nietzsche. Based on current evidence, the statement origin seems to be anonymous. Quote Investigator, "Those Who Dance."

My colleague was gobsmacked, reflecting, "In my parish work (a large local church), parishioners would have their differences and carry them for months. These people are such an example with their forgiveness and how we should live."

In a psychogeriatric ward, Mavis, tall, thin, insect-like, was rattling the plastic table that restrained her in her chair. "Help, help," was her feeble cry. It was heartbreaking to see such an independent, well-educated person reduced to this.

"What's up, Mavis?" I sat next to her, my hand lightly on her arm. Mavis is practically blind. "I'm Rosemarie, the chaplain."

"Please can you help me out of here? I can't get up. It's awful; I feel so trapped. I want to go for a swim."

"Mavis, this table is here to keep you safe, so you don't fall again; you had a nasty injury last time," the passing nurse reminded her.

Mavis looked at me intently. "What's the point of living like this? I'd rather fall over; I can't bear it; I feel so trapped. I just want to go for a swim."

"I know, Mavis; it is terrible not to have that freedom—I would hate it too. Did you grow up by the beach?" "Yes." "And so did I—we both have sand in our souls." She liked that. She enjoyed words, I recall. "Would you like me to read you something?"

I read to her from Eccl 3, and she sat there transfixed. She then began to stutter with emotion. "That is beautiful; please read it again." This time, she repeated the words with me; she was much calmer now.

We were joined by Trixie, a young nurse. In contrast to her eighty-five-year-old patient, Trixie was only twenty-three. She crouched down beside Mavis. "Rosemarie, I've been wanting to talk to you. My mother died a couple of months ago." "I'm so sorry, Trixie—I didn't know that." "She committed suicide." "Oh, Trixie, that's terrible for you." I was shocked.

It was then that I noticed Mavis's hand reaching blindly out toward Trixie's head. She felt her hair and began to stroke it, so very gently. "That is awful," she said. "You are so young to lose your mother." The tears began to trickle down Trixie's cheeks as she looked up helplessly to Mavis. It was a tender moment.

I became the observer. "Treat people as if they were what they ought to be and you help them to become what they are capable of being."[23]

Trixie revealed that her natural father had abandoned her. "He didn't want me." Mavis continued to stroke Trixie's hair, to feel the tears streaming down her cheeks, gently encouraging her with "the strength I have seen in you," and at the same time acknowledging the enormity of her loss. It was a most appropriate interaction—one of compassion and sensitivity and love—a window of normality in a dementing woman's downward spiral.

Mavis was meeting Trixie's need for nurturing with the life-wisdom and heart of someone who had never been a mother—a dementing elderly woman who had been rattling her chair tray and calling, "Help, help, I want to go for a swim." And now she was swimming! Her release was in the moment—finding meaning and purpose.

Mavis's prayer from a recent chapel service came to mind—"*I pray that I might not become useless.*" God uses broken vessels[24]—sometimes a connection comes in the least expected way!

At a community based residential mental health facility, during my visit with students Rowena and Zelda, resident Paul offered to play the piano, and fetched chairs for his guests.

> I recalled the first time he had played for me—with such a maestro flourish. His nimble fingers ran up and down the piano with no tune at all—but it was a great performance. "Where did you learn to play like that?" I asked after applauding him. "Oh," he said, "I saw someone on TV playing the piano like that, and I thought, 'I can do that!' And so I did!"

---

23. A quote generally attributed to Johann Wolfgang von Goethe. Burk, "To See the Best."

24. "But we have this treasure in earthen vessels, that the excellency of the power may be of God, and not us" (2 Cor 4:7 KJV). The treasure within us is his Holy Spirit and it is exposed best through brokenness.

I felt sad when, as we departed, the students were laughing about Paul and his bizarre performance. I decided to share a little of his story to give them some insight.

> Paul had to be dragged from his home many years ago when the neighbors objected to his hoarding. While he lived with no electricity, he had a huge collection of old car parts in his garden. He has always grieved for the loss of the place where he belonged.
>
> In his previous ward, where he had been for many years, he fed the birds and watered the flowers—it gave meaning and purpose to his life. He was known as "always the gentleman," serving people, and insisting "ladies first." He cried when other residents died. They were his family.
>
> When transferred to this present facility, he had to be dragged away from his second home. Paul was a skinny little man, but "It took six big nurses," he recalled. "I could have flattened them, but I wanted to preserve their dignity."

Rowena became emotional when she shared her written reflections with me in individual supervision. She realized that Paul owned nothing excepting his piano performance—that was his identity, and it was the gift that he offered, along with his hospitality, to those who visit. Inspired by his example of resilience and boldness, Rowena decided to take a risk with her strong reluctance to lead a chapel service. She announced, "If Paul can perform, so can I! He's encouraged me to be free to be me without embarrassment." I applauded Rowena's growing self-confidence, which was one of her goals. Transformational learning is the magic of CPE!

The irony is that CPE was founded in a psychiatric hospital in the 1920s by Anton Boisen[25] in order to teach theological students how to be relevant. However, in recent decades, training in mental health ministry has been seen as optional by chaplains and by the church.

But . . . *specialized training and supervision is needed* for ethical mental health ministry[26] as its intricacies, complexities, and

---

25. Holifield, "Boisen," 104.
26. Bogia, "Mental Health Chaplaincy," 717.

subtleties require experienced handling so as to "do no harm,"[27] not only to others, but, importantly, also to self.

First, "know thyself."[28] While it's important to "be where they are at," it's vital first to be self-aware—of who you are and where you're coming from—otherwise you can get lost in other people's worlds.

Parker Palmer tells us, "There was a time when farmers on the Great Plains, at the first sign of a blizzard, would run a rope from the back door out to the barn. They all knew stories of people who had wandered off and been frozen to death, having lost sight of home in a whiteout while still in their own backyards."[29]

Action-reflection learning is the core of CPE. As Socrates observed, "The unexamined life is not worth living."[30] Students are always accompanied by a supervisor who demonstrates a safe, effective, and respectful way of working and encourages them to reflect. Learning "on the job" gives stimulation, enjoyment, and confidence to students who might feel "I'm always ready to learn, although I do not always like being taught."[31] Learning becomes transformational, enabling students to grow and blossom fully in their God-created uniqueness.

THE MUTUALITY OF SUPERVISION

While I have authority[32] in my pastoral experience and expertise, there is danger after twenty-five years of becoming stagnant, and

---

27. It is often said that the exact phrase "First do no harm" (Latin, *Primum non nocere*) is a part of the original Hippocratic oath. Although the phrase does not appear in the AD 245 version of the oath, similar intentions are vowed by, "I will abstain from all intentional wrong-doing and harm." Wikipedia, "Hippocratic Oath."

28. "Know thyself" is a philosophical maxim which was inscribed upon the Temple of Apollo in the ancient Greek precinct of Delphi.

29. Palmer, *Hidden Wholeness*, 1.

30. Wikipedia, "Unexamined Life."

31. Quote by Winston S. Churchill (Nov. 4, 1952, while speaking in the House of Commons in London). Quote Investigator, "Always Ready to Learn."

32. Hawkins and Shohet, *Supervision*, 113.

so I try to have a "beginner's mind"[33]—emptied, and open. There are lessons inherent in every interaction, and sometimes I miss the subtleties that fresh eyes see.

"In everyone's life at some time, our inner fire goes out. It is then burst into flame by an encounter with another human being. We should all be thankful for those people who rekindle the human spirit."[34] Accompanying students as they visit these wards and then sharing in their reflections are the "light bulb moments" that enrich my practice.

THE ANXIETY OF NOT KNOWING

"Genuine dialogue means a surrender of authority to uncertainty."[35] There is a liberation and aliveness in this approach that Mezirow addresses. He recommends that we, as supervisors, see our role as "not so much to profess as to facilitate," and to accept that "everyone becomes a teacher and a learner."[36]

Grover Criswell tells a well-known Hasidic story:

> After stumbling around for a while, [they] come upon a man who has been lost there even longer. They all jump up and down and get excited. . . . Finally someone who can tell them how to get out of here, a man with answers. With a humility, echoing the best of CPE supervision, the wise old man responds that he doesn't know the way out. He, too, lives with the anxiety of not knowing. He does know where some thickets are. He has been lost in them. He does know where some bushes are that scratch and wound. He has the scars. "Maybe," he invites them,

---

33. *Shoshin* (Japanese) is a concept from Zen Buddhism meaning beginner's mind. It refers to having an attitude of openness, eagerness, and lack of preconceptions.

34. The quoted passage is from one of many translations over the decades of Albert Schweitzer's 1924 memoir *Aus meiner Kindheit und Jugendzeit* (*Memoirs of Childhood and Youth*). Quote Investigator, "Inner Fire."

35. Mandell and Herman, "When Learners Make the Learning," 80.

36. Mandell and Herman, "When Learners Make the Learning," 79–80.

"if we journey together we can find our way, but at the very least, we will have each other."[37]

CONFRONTING THE DARKNESS

Too many of us panic in the dark. We don't understand that it's a holy dark and that the idea is to surrender to it and journey through to real light."[38]

In the double-locked intensive care psychiatric unit I meet the people who are most deeply distressed and disturbed. They have no freedom; they may have no possessions—not even their own clothes. Some may become angry and abusive—likely to harm themselves or others.

Yet . . . here are my most profound, sacred, and privileged moments of ministry when I see tough, remorseless men drop to their knees, weeping in prayer. As one of these men said to me, "This is how we stand before God—with nothing." One day, as we were leaving, a young, disheveled man farewelled us with, "Thank you for visiting us when everyone else has forgotten us."

This is why I do what I do. It's about making a difference. And, while I know that I hold the Christ-light of hope in the corridors of darkness, I also know that I have the privilege of meeting Jesus in the people who are imprisoned there. For he said, "I was in prison and you came to visit me" (Matt 25:36). This is holy ground. *This is mental health ministry!*

BIBLIOGRAPHY

Bogia, Benjamin P. "Mental Health Chaplaincy." In *Dictionary of Pastoral Care and Counseling*, edited by Rodney J. Hunter et al., 717. Nashville: Abingdon, 1990.

Boisen, Anton T. *The Exploration of the Inner World*. New York: Willet, Clark, 1936.

37. Hemenway, *Inside the Circle*, 84.
38. Kidd, *When the Heart Waits*, 152.

Brown, Brené. *The Gifts of Imperfection: Let Go of Who You Think You're Supposed to Be and Embrace Who You Are*. Center City, MN: Hazelden, 2010.

Burk, George J. "To See the Best in Others Will Help Them Become the Best." TapRoot, Aug. 26, 2014. https://taproot.com/to-see-the-best-in-others-will-help-them-become-the-best.

Carson, Marion L. S. *The Pastoral Care of People with Mental Health Problems*. London: SPCK, 2008.

De Mello, Anthony. *The Song of the Bird*. Anand, India: Gujarat Sahitya Prakash, 1989.

Hawkins, Peter, and Robin Shohet. *Supervision in the Helping Professions*. 3rd ed. Maidenhead, UK: Open University, 2006.

Hemenway, Joan E. *Inside the Circle: A Historical and Practical Inquiry Concerning Process Groups in Clinical Pastoral Education*. Decatur, GA: Journal of Pastoral Care, 1995.

Holifield, E. Brooks. "Boisen." In *Dictionary of Pastoral Care and Counseling*, edited by Rodney J. Hunter et al., 104–5. Nashville: Abingdon, 1990.

Kelly, Ewen. *Personhood and Presence*. London: T&T Clark International, 2012.

Kidd, Sue Monk. *When the Heart Waits: Spiritual Direction for Life's Sacred Questions*. New York: HarperCollins, 2006.

Kirschenbaum, Howard, and Valerie Land Henderson, eds. *Carl Rogers—Dialogues: Conversations with Martin Buber, Paul Tillich, B. F. Skinner, Gregory Bateson, Michael Polanyi, Rollo May, and Others*. London: Constable and Robinson, 1990.

Lowthorpe, Philippa, dir. *Call the Midwife*. Season 1, episode 1, "Episode #1.1." Aired Jan. 15, 2012, on ABC iview.

Mackay, Hugh. *What Makes Us Tick? The Ten Desires That Drive Us*. Sydney: Hachette Australia, 2010.

Mandell, Alan, and Lee Herman. "Mentoring: When Learners Make the Learning." In *Transformative Learning in Practice: Insights from Community, Workplace, and Higher Education*, edited by Jack Mezirow et al., 78–88. San Francisco: Jossey-Bass, 2009.

Merton, Thomas. *Conjectures of a Guilty Bystander*. New York: Bantam Doubleday Dell, 1994.

Mocerino, Rosella [Blue, pseud.]. "Edvard Munch: Reflections on Life and Death." *The Painter's Eye* (blog), Mar. 19, 2023. https://www.thepainterseye.com/post/edvard-munch-reflections-on-life-and-death.

Palmer, Parker J. *A Hidden Wholeness: The Journey Toward an Undivided Life*. San Francisco: Jossey-Bass, 2004.

Quote Investigator. "Quote Origin: I Am Always Ready to Learn, Although I Do Not Always Like Being Taught." July 24, 2012. https://quoteinvestigator.com/2012/07/24/ready-to-learn.

———. "Quote Origin: Sometimes Our Inner Fire Goes Out. Another Person Rekindles It and Deserves Our Deepest Gratitude." Nov. 8, 2023. https://quoteinvestigator.com/2023/11/08/rekindle-fire.

———. "Quote Origin: Those Who Dance Are Considered Insane by Those Who Can't Hear the Music." June 5, 2012. https://quoteinvestigator.com/2012/06/05/dance-insane.

Rogers, Carl R. *On Becoming a Person*. Boston: Houghton Mifflin, 1961.

Truth About Nursing. "The Nightingale Pledge." https://www.truthaboutnursing.org/press/pioneers/nightingale_pledge.html#gsc.tab=0.

Wikipedia. "Hippocratic Oath." Last modified Nov. 23, 2024. https://en.wikipedia.org/wiki/Hippocratic_Oath.

———. "Know Thyself." Last modified Nov. 26, 2024. https://en.wikipedia.org/wiki/Know_thyself.

———. "The Unexamined Life Is Not Worth Living." Last modified Jan. 20, 2025. https://en.wikipedia.org/wiki/The_unexamined_life_is_not_worth_living.

10

Reflective Believing

A New Name, Not a New Method

SUSANNE SCHMIDT

> If you talk to a [person] in a language [they] understand that goes to [their] head. If you talk to [them] in [their] language that goes to [their] heart.
>
> —Nelson Mandela

INTRODUCTION

Several years ago, just after achieving my CPE supervisor-educator level, I was invited to give a presentation to my colleagues at an education weekend. I was somewhat taken aback, feeling very junior still within the group. However, on reflection, my interest in new spiritualities and, in particular, new ways of looking at the reflective process within the CPE program had been recognized by my peers and I had been invited to speak about this. In the ensuing years, I have continued to work further on this and come to understand and believe that the reflective component is where the genius of CPE lies. It does however need to be responsive to the times, places, and people both that it educates and that it serves. This chapter is my response to new spiritualities and ways of reflecting. It will look at how the reflective process of CPE, traditionally called "theological reflection," can retain its heart and wisdom by moving to a new name and slight nuancing of practice that captures the zeitgeist of students entering into the CPE process, the people to whom they will be attending and the systems that will be employing them, and how they understand the work of spiritual care. It will look at Australian data in the spiritual and pastoral space to support this and include current spiritual and theological thought in the CPE space, some recent sociological research in this area, and some educative and supervisory theory to support this.

RELIGION IN AUSTRALIA

The most recent census data available[1] puts Christianity at just over 43 percent of the population with Catholics making up the largest subset of this at just over 20 percent. These have reduced by 20 percent and 13 percent respectively since the last census. The group reporting no religion sits at 40 percent, effectively doubling in the last ten years. Australians in the "other" groupings include Islam at 2.6 percent, the same as the previous census, and Hinduism at 2.7 percent, a relatively small raw number but a 55.3 percent increase on the previous census. Interestingly, the religion question has been in every census since its inception—it is the only "voluntary" question—and in the 2021 census, the number of people electing to answer it increased from 91 percent to 93 percent.

When CPE first started as a training method in the US in the early part of the twentieth century, the 1911 Australian census put Christianity at 96 percent of the population. This has enormous implications for how the training of pastoral carers might reflect the circumstances of the people they find themselves interacting with and also the backgrounds that they themselves come from. In

1. Australian Bureau of Statistics, "2021 Census."

my territory of Canberra, the 2021 census shows it has the lowest percentage of Christian affiliations, the highest (along with NSW), by a significant factor, of people reporting in the main "other" group (Islam, Judaism, Hinduism, Buddhism), and of the "no religion" affiliates it is the second highest to SA at around 45 percent, five percentage points below Tasmania.[2] While I have never taught an atheist in my CPE groups over the twelve years I have been supervising, I have taught a mixture of the mainline Christian traditions, a number of evangelical Christians, one Hindu, a number of Buddhists, one Muslim, one Spiritualist, and several that would self-identify as spiritual but not religious (SBNR). One of my CPE colleagues training a few years below me identifies as Hare Krishna. While the very nature of spiritual and pastoral care training in Australia tends to attract people who would trend toward the more traditionally religious end of the spectrum, increasingly, certainly anecdotally, students are coming to CPE courses from a wider variety of spiritual backgrounds, and this has strong influences on the life experiences, educational backgrounds, and understandings they bring to the course.

SPIRITUALITY IN AUSTRALIA

Spiritual Health Association, the peak body in Australia lobbying for the advocacy and promotion of spiritual care in the health sector, commissioned a report conducted by McCrindle Research on the benefits and future of spiritual care in the Australian health sector (the McCrindle survey).[3] This dovetails in with my own research findings.[4] McCrindle's generationally, religiously, spiritually, and culturally diverse survey of over twenty-five hundred people found that people believed that spirituality was essential to mental, relational, and physical well-being.[5] It found that

2. Australian Bureau of Statistics, "Snapshot of Australia."
3. Spiritual Health Association, *Future of Spiritual Care*.
4. Lobb et al., "Patient Reported Outcomes"; Snowden et al., "What's On Your Mind?"
5. Spiritual Health Association, *Future of Spiritual Care*, 4.

people nominated that spirituality offered peace, values, morality, purpose, and love.[6] People who had received spiritual care in a hospital felt confident, supported, and comforted by it.[7] Barriers to spiritual care in health included the patient not feeling confident in talking about spiritual matters and not having a private space.[8] Interestingly, qualifications were seen as important in the person being spoken to, but the profession of spiritual care practitioner ranked well below other professionals such as psychologist and counselor in a number of generational groups[9] which suggests the profession has some work to do in this area.

My own study backs these findings—that when people had a visit from a pastoral carer, the patients felt they could be honest with themselves, with a sense of peace, a better perspective of their illness, less anxiety, and felt more in control. The patient was able to talk about what was on their mind and this aspect in particular was of great value, specifically the calm, non-anxious, and reflective stance of the person that was doing the listening. This was regardless of the stated religious or spiritual stance of the patient which was factored into the research output. The McCrindle survey defines that spirituality has many expressions in Australia, and in order for a spiritual care practitioner to be effective they need to be able to work with how this is manifested.[10]

The days of "the chaplain" only visiting people from their own tradition are fast vanishing in many spaces in Australia. Today's CPE student needs to be effective and responsive in meeting the spiritual needs of however it is expressed in the encounter they have.

---

6. Spiritual Health Association, *Future of Spiritual Care*, 12.
7. Spiritual Health Association, *Future of Spiritual Care*, 15.
8. Spiritual Health Association, *Future of Spiritual Care*, 18.
9. Spiritual Health Association, *Future of Spiritual Care*, 17.
10. Spiritual Health Association, *Future of Spiritual Care*, 8. The McCrindle survey was based on a similar survey done by the Fetzer Institute in the US. See appendix for a pictogram of how their survey summarized expressions of spirituality.

EDUCATION THEORY

While it can be suggested that this is the core business of the CPE process, transformative education theory generally (the ability to adjust ideas based on new education, e.g., Mezirow and others) would contend that it is important in any area of adult education. The CPE "trust the process" maxim asks the student to continually look at their own foundational beliefs, how they hold them within the pastoral encounter, and whether they support the process of supporting the other. The effective supervisor is asked to do this also through the process of regular and self-supervision. Willis and Leiman call this a "pedagogy of the heart."

> We contend that an education of the heart requires an exploration and deepening of both the teacher's and the student's core myths . . . a balance between a pedagogy that nurtures the student's . . . choice which is assumed to be grounded in their personal myths . . . while simultaneously providing them with a sound critique of the social system along with the knowledge necessary for ethical practice.[11]

This type of knowledge is insight-formed and based on shared human experience, and, while they are speaking about higher education generally, they have tapped into the wisdom of the reflective process of the pastoral encounter in CPE. Their idea of a heart-based pedagogy also reflects Parker Palmer's hospitality-based sharing of stories where the smaller story of the student taps into the larger story of the discipline and the tradition.[12] And, again, this speaks to the heart of the imaginative process that reflection at its best can be in the reflective encounter of the PER ("Pastoral Encounter Report," formerly verbatim)—How can the student reflect on their story in the light of the patient encounter and in the light of the greater tradition and wisdom, both of their own story and the greater one of the world in which they are situated? Then, how can they take this out with them into their next

---

11. Willis and Leiman, "Pedagogy of the Heart," 661.
12. Willis and Leiman, "Pedagogy of the Heart," 663.

encounter with a greater understanding of self and practice? Willis and Leiman, drawing on the work of Parker Palmer, identify these tasks as *naming, listening, integrating,* and *hospitality*.[13]

SUPERVISORY THEORY

Michael Carroll's theories[14] around supervision for transformational learning dovetail beautifully into the reflective practice component of CPE and the idea of a pedagogy of the heart for wisdom-based practice. He explores theories of education where the supervisor works with uncertainty (transformative theory) and hospitable accommodation within the reflective process in order to facilitate discovery. This involves leaving the comfort zone of one story to enter into another. Within CPE, this can be found in a number of places, and for this chapter I want to explore these concepts of transformation and hospitable accommodation and creativity with the specific aspect of what has traditionally been called theological reflection.

REFLECTIVE BELIEVING[15]

(Note that I will use the term *theological reflection* (TR) until I explain why I will stop using it.) Mildred Best in her essay on the process of TR in the teaching of CPE speaks of it being the essence of what is done in CPE and of what distinguishes it from other helping professions.[16] She writes about it enabling the student to notice who they are in the world in relation to the other and quotes Barth as it being the process of reflecting with "the Bible in one hand and the newspaper (modern equivalent—mobile phone!) in

---

13. Willis and Leiman, "Pedagogy of the Heart," 669.

14. Carroll, "Supervision," 210–17.

15. I have worked extensively with this idea over about six years of CPE teaching and based my work largely on the initial ideas of Edward Foley and his concept of "reflective believing." See Foley, "Reflective Believing."

16. Best, "Reflecting Theologically," 16.

the other."[17] She says that it helps students to consider the interrelatedness between themselves, others, and God and what it means to be created in God's image.[18] While I agree that TR is the key to the CPE process and a distinguishing feature, and its interrelatedness between the student and things outside them are all vital, it is the use of God and Bible that site TR firmly in Christianity that make TR problematic for a postmodern era. The challenge is to take the genius and uniqueness of the TR process and re-form it for the spiritual lives of both the students and those for whom they are being equipped to work for into the future. This may involve its traditional God-based theological focus for those for whom this is foundational, and it may reach into newer areas of spirituality for others for whom Christianity is not their propositional stance.

Language is not neutral. If I (Susanne/female/she/her) lead a meeting, I am not the chairman. Words that meant something in one context now mean something different and are used differently, sometimes generationally (e.g., pussy, gay, midget, and fag, just to cite a few). If you do not have teens or young adults, then *boujie* and *stonks* are probably a foreign language to you. Many of us may struggle to use *they* as a singular pronoun for gender identity. Religious language is part of this. The word *theology*, according to Thomas Aquinas, is a discipline that is wholly and solely of God.[19] So for the Buddhist or the Hindu or Jew or the seeker, how can they work with a term that may have little or no impact for them? Foley would argue that the prevailing understanding was that "everyone" would use the term and Jews would nuance it G-d, etc., and then Muslims would nuance it slightly more, and then Buddhists slightly more, and then everyone else would work in the next layer out. What this did however was that it centralized the Christian understanding of theo-God and logos-word as the norm and everyone else as needing to work out of some sort of nuancing of this norm. Similar ideas exist in feminist theory

17. Best, "Reflecting Theologically," 15.

18. Best, "Reflecting Theologically," 13.

19. Starling, "What Is Theology" (a definition from Morling College that references Aquinas's *Summa Theologiae*).

and in theories around ethically competent supervision in racial matters that can tend to work out of male and white frameworks either consciously or unconsciously, because they have been the prevailing frameworks for centuries.[20]

However, census figures demonstrate the diversity of belief systems that operate in both our CPE groups and in the world in which they work. Our CPE teaching needs a framework that can reflect this both as input (group members) and output (the places where spiritual care practitioners will be working).

The traditional and simplest model of TR asks the student to begin with the experience (the patient encounter), to explore this in the light of what sustains them (traditions/beliefs/values), and then to reflect on this in the light of the above with implications for future practice. My premise is that while TR is designed to focus on the practitioner and not the subject/patient, a random survey of CPE 1 students would suggest that they focus mostly on the belief system of the patient rather than what was happening for them as practitioner in the encounter—and the word *theological* is the barrier. It is a barrier for those students who come out of Christian traditions and have some theological training because they tend to go straight for a head response, go to their concordance, and inevitably end up in the book of Job with quotes on suffering, bringing it back to the patient and not their own felt response. It is also difficult for those students who do not have a "God/god" in their spiritual or support system, for whom the word theology has little or no meaning. Asking them to "translate" asks them to accept a dominant paradigm whose systems have the first right and their own are secondary. There is a cultural arrogance in this and it is not hospitable to the other.

Reflective believing (RB) as a concept was developed by US professor of spirituality and liturgy Edward Foley as a result of a fifteen-month sabbatical and extensive consultation in the field of

20. This chapter does not have the capacity to delve into the nuances of these very interesting side topics; however, there is some thought-provoking writing, particularly out of the US, around reflective practice in the #blacklivesmatter space, and gender power dynamics are an issue every supervisor needs to be aware of.

theological and pastoral education. He based it on students who were enrolling through pastoral education units and data of patients in hospitals as well as extensive consultation with professionals and organizations in the field. It is not a new method as the process of reflecting on the encounter in the light of personal belief systems and then learning from these was core to the process. As Foley notes, "Not a new method but a new language game for the reflective art."[21]

Foley chose the word *reflective* because the process of reflection is key to the need for anyone working with their own belief systems to be able to examine what it is that holds them. This is the core of any theory of supervision. It is the core of what is taught in CPE. He chose believing because everyone has a belief system—belief in God, the other, nature, their family, their football team. They act out of this system. He calls it "a linguistic currency worth harvesting."[22]

Interestingly, too, he went from the adjective/noun combination of TR to the adverb/verb combination of RB as he suggests this makes the participant far more active in the process, and spoke of the dynamism inherent in this.

PHILOSOPHY OF HOSPITALITY IN THE REFLECTIVE SPACE

As a hospitable supervisor, I create a welcome space where the other can feel safe to explore. RB allows for creativity, respect, courage, and cultural humility that says there are multiple languages and ways of meaning making in the world.

In my practice, I introduce many different models of reflection. I begin with teaching the traditional TR model. I am still deciding if I want to move away from this completely. I also call this model *spiritual reflection* (SR) and invite students to choose the heading they feel speaks to them more closely. I then introduce RB

---

21. Foley, "Reflective Believing," 70.
22. Foley, "Reflective Believing," 69.

and offer it up as a third alternative[23]—and some students choose this one. I model and use different process models of reflection such as the sand tray method and picture card method. I encourage students to use images, texts from literature, and the great writings of the world as their exemplars when writing their TR/SR/RB. I am aware of students' learning styles and try and work both within them and around them to create new learning pathways that might help them to explore what might be unknown to them (aka the Johari window). RB encourages the practice to be an art form, which promotes flexibility, so sometimes I improvise. I have found the sand tray method in particular to be very insightful in group supervision for religiously conservative students. These methods can be used for individual supervision as well.

With a student who came from a conservative Christian background and often felt a pastoral encounter to be a fail if nothing religious was mentioned and whose TRs always used Bible texts, he became stuck in working with a PER. I asked him if he was willing to try something different. I asked him to look around the very bare room we were sitting in and see if there was anything that spoke to him of how he felt in the encounter he was presenting. He chose the room's emergency escape plan. A very insightful RB then ensued, which allowed him to move from his very intellectual TR that he had written to a much more intuitive and relationally based one based on his gut instinct of wanting to escape from the patient who was speaking about deep emotional matters. It enabled this student to be able to see his capability wider than just as a religious pastoral carer.

Hospitality requires me to both hold students safe within boundaries yet know how flexible those boundaries can be. It requires me to have knowledge of and be welcoming of the wide variety of spiritual belief systems in postmodern Australia that students will be bringing into the group, how these support them, how they will work with these to support others, and how I will supervise them around this.

---

23. The full model in Foley's papers has a more extensive list of pointers that assist an understanding of it.

Reflective believing allows us to share our wisdom and our humanity for the common good of the other.

> The real magic of discovery lies not in seeing new landscapes but in having new eyes.
>
> —Marcel Proust

APPENDIX

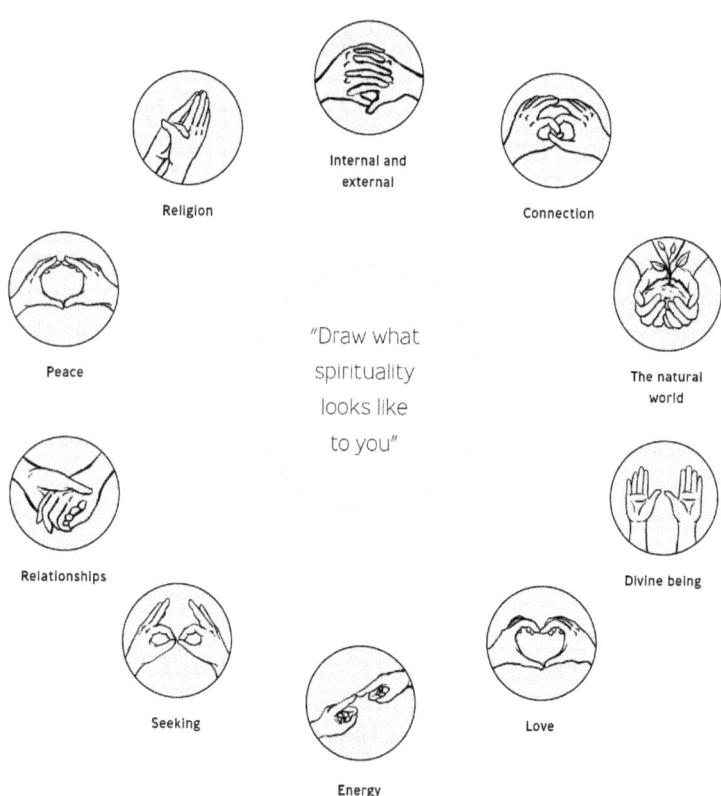

What Does Spirituality Mean to You? Reprinted with permission from the Fetzer Institute.[24]

24. Selzler et al., *Study of Spirituality*, 13.

BIBLIOGRAPHY

Australian Bureau of Statistics. "2021 Census Shows Changes in Australia's Religious Diversity." June 28, 2022. https://www.abs.gov.au/media-centre/media-releases/2021-census-shows-changes-australias-religious-diversity.

———. "Snapshot of Australia." June 28, 2022. https://www.abs.gov.au/statistics/people/people-and-communities/snapshot-australia/latest-release.

Best, Mildred. "Reflecting Theologically." In *Courageous Conversations: The Teaching and Learning of Pastoral Supervision*, edited by William R. DeLong, 13–20. Lanham, MD: University Press of America, 2010.

Carroll, Michael. "Supervision: Critical Reflection for Transformational Learning, Part 1." *Clinical Supervisor* 28 (2009) 210–20.

Foley, Edward. "Reflective Believing: Reimagining Theological Reflection in an Age of Diversity." *Reflective Practice: Formation and Supervision in Ministry* 34 (2014) 60–75.

Lobb, Elizabeth A., et al. "Patient Reported Outcomes of Pastoral Care in a Hospital Setting." *Journal of Health Care Chaplaincy* 25 (2019) 131–46.

Selzler, Veronica, et al. *What Does Spirituality Mean to Us? A Study of Spirituality in the United States*. Fetzer Institute, Sept. 2020. https://fetzer.org/resources/what-does-spirituality-mean-us-study-spirituality-united-states.

Snowden, Austyn, et al. "'What's On Your Mind?' The Only Necessary Question in Spiritual Care." *Journal for the Study of Spirituality* 8 (2018) 19–33.

Spiritual Health Association. *The Future of Spiritual Care in Australia: A National Study on Spirituality, Wellbeing and Spiritual Care in Hospitals*. Dec. 2021. https://spiritualhealth.org.au/resource/the-future-of-spiritual-care-in-australia.

Starling, David. "What Is Theology and Why Should I Study It?" *Morling College* (blog), Dec. 10, 2018. https://www.morling.edu.au/blog/what-is-theology.

Willis, Eileen, and Tania Leiman. "In Defence of a Pedagogy of the Heart: Theory and Practice in the Use of Imaginal Knowledge." *Higher Education Research and Development* 32 (2013) 660–71.

11

Vulnerability in Cross-Cultural Supervision
MARY PEARSON

INTRODUCTION

It is important, at the start, to clarify where I sit culturally: I am a white woman who emigrated from Scotland to Aotearoa New Zealand in my middle years. The fact that I use the term *Aotearoa* is significant because it denotes a shift in consciousness. It was a shocking discovery to realize that I was now identified with colonizers and settlers. Living in a different hemisphere, "Down Under," changed my focus in more ways than one. I had only a vague notion of the Pacific region but now had the opportunity to learn a little about Māori culture and make friends with several Pacific Islanders. They brought a glimpse of cultural, community, and family life that was different. These learnings were compounded on moving to Australia. Here I found myself part of an even more painful story of colonization and evident ongoing injustice and powerlessness for Indigenous Australians. The impact of these migrations for me was in having to recognize how little I knew or understood. I was also surrounded by very many other migrants about whose cultures I knew little. I became very aware of my "whiteness." It was humbling.

VULNERABILITY AND POWER

This awareness was destabilizing. Hand in hand with it has come a recognition of vulnerability. As a supervisor, I thought that vulnerability related to the potential power differential between myself as the white person and a supervisee from a non-Western background. There may well be an unacknowledged power that is held by those from the dominant "white" background. Peter Hawkins and Robin Shohet note that "imbalances of power are inevitably played out in professional relationships including the relationship between supervisee and supervisor and between supervisee and client."[1] Another more hidden aspect of power and consequent vulnerability however is aversive racism: I might think I am acting with an open mind and good intentions, but, in fact, may be subconsciously belittling my supervisee.[2]

JOURNEYING TOWARD AWARENESS

I have come to see that vulnerability in cross-cultural supervision lies firstly with the supervisor because of the need for honest self-awareness. Hawkins explains the need to come with "an openness to others, a difference which is free from preconceptions and fixed opinions."[3] Shohet talks about our core beliefs: "At the heart of my work as a supervisor is examining core beliefs."[4] If we do not, the risk is that "in attaching to core beliefs we try to make the world fit our belief systems."[5] White, Western people have a particular responsibility. Hawkins and Shohet state, "White, Western people

---

1. Hawkins and Shohet, *Supervision*, 111.
2. Aversive racism is defined by John Dovodio and Samuel Gaertner as "a form of prejudice characterizing the thoughts, feelings, and behaviors of the majority of well-intentioned and ostensibly nonprejudiced" citizens. Pearson, "Imagining," 22.
3. Hawkins, "Foreword," 9.
4. Shohet, "Fear and Love in Supervision," 190.
5. Shohet, "Fear and Love in Supervision," 192.

tend to see themselves as culturally neutral."[6] This believed neutrality is deeply problematic, as Robin DiAngelo, writing as a white woman in North America, explains. "Given how seldom we experience racial discomfort in a society we dominate, we haven't had to build up our racial stamina. Socialized into a deeply internalized sense of superiority that we are either unaware of or can never admit to ourselves, we become highly fragile in conversations about race."[7] Fragility compounds lack of awareness beneath which lie individual formative and companion experiences, habits of thinking, and unconscious and unavoidable biases that we carry into any cross-cultural encounter. DiAngelo elaborates on how fragility leads to denial of any racist thinking. Denial is described by Mark DeYmaz as the start of a continuum of cross-cultural competency. Cultural blindness follows, after which a tipping point is reached that can shift into awareness. Eventually competency may be achieved, which is not an end point. It can never be fully achieved.[8]

If we can overcome fragility and accept vulnerability, with growing awareness we may uncover unconscious feelings of superiority or begin to see how privilege and security have formed us, if we were fortunate. We are all the centers of our own world and may fall into what Rodney Fopp names as *ethnocentrism*, in which "one response is to ignore the possibility that our own cultural background influences how we see other cultural beliefs and practices, to assume (presume is a less neutral but probably more accurate word) that our culture is the benchmark by which we should judge all others."[9] We may be suspicious of different religious practices and lack understanding about the extent to which culture and religion may be connected, uncertain if they can be separated.[10]

---

6. Hawkins and Shohet, *Supervision*, 104.
7. DiAngelo, *White Fragility*, 2.
8. DeYmaz, *Building*, 103.
9. Fopp, *Enhancing Understanding*, 10.
10. Fopp, *Enhancing Understanding*, 12.

LOCATING DIFFERENCE

It is important to state what is, hopefully, obvious—that not all difference is related to culture. Hawkins and Shohet, writing about supervising across difference, point to three different ways of responding to culture: The universalist who "denies the importance of culture and puts difference down to individual characteristics"; the particularist who puts "all difference down to culture"; and the transcendentalist who views "both the client and the counsellor [as having] vast experiences that deeply influence their worldviews and behaviour."[11]

NEUTRALITY AND UNDERSTANDING

We begin to see that supervision is not culturally neutral. This does not mean that we are not wholeheartedly committed to regarding everyone as of equal value, nor that we would knowingly disrespect others. We may feel, because we are open minded, indeed are keen to be so, that we can understand. We want to understand. The danger is that, as Fopp says, "even when we disagree with other cultures and their values or outlook, we take for granted that we can understand them."[12] Paradoxically, fear of not understanding can become a barrier. We worry about failing to connect because we do not understand. What emerges is our vulnerability as supervisors. Shohet says, "We have a very deep need to connect, and fear gets in our way. It is the biggest block to intimacy and communication."[13]

Fundamentally, supervision remains a relational space. We hope to create space for what Julie Hewson calls "the generosity of heart, sharing, resourcing, empathy and accord."[14] As supervisors, we are trained to listen and hear behind the words. In supervision with people from a somewhat similar background we may make

11. Hawkins and Shohet, *Supervision*, 105.
12. Fopp, *Enhancing Understanding*, 1.
13. Shohet, "Fear and Love in Supervision," 189.
14. Hewson, "Passionate Supervision," 42.

assumptions because we find unconscious points of connection. In cross-cultural supervision, we may realize that there is a gap because there is difference.

CROSSING OVER THE GAPS

Cross-cultural supervision implies a crossing over, a bridging of gaps. There is a distinction between this and the term *inter-cultural* which implies a flow of ideas, a seeking out of shared values and a movement toward commonality. The word *cross* carries theological significance. It implies a point of intersection between the human and the divine; a place of vulnerability, of pain and of self-denial, of preparedness to take up one's cross. While it may seem fraught with difficulty, crossing over the gaps is an invitation into a new space. Empathy is often considered a virtue in this situation, but Lydia Johnstone helpfully describes "interpathy," where "we fully enter another worldview, bracketing our own cultural values temporarily so that we can actually participate, in some sense, in the alien world."[15]

Interpathy recognizes the gap even while it may not be fully understood; differences are respected. Fopp highlights that "the value we assign to other cultures influences how we learn about them."[16] For example, we might ask ourselves what weight people from a Western background give to the connection to family and community of Pacific Island cultures, where the self, the "I" or "me" is secondary to the "we" and "our." We might reflect on how much the evident greater formality and respect for older people in Asian cultures is recognized. Are the oral traditions of Indigenous and Pacific cultures, where people are more used to sitting and listening, valued and respected? In Tongan culture there is a name for the space of listening and learning: the *vā*.[17] It is a sacred relational space; sacred because within it there is respect for the

---

15. Johnson, *Drinking From the Same Well*, 60.
16. Fopp, *Enhancing Understanding*, 36.
17. Tu'iono, "Seeking to Create 'Vā' Spaces."

other and a recognition that room should be made to allow for difference. There are connections between the *vā* and the supervision space that can be useful to ponder.

With all such thoughts in our heads, we might enter the supervision space feeling quite inadequate to the task. Yet that vulnerability can be a gift within the power dynamics of cross-cultural supervision. As Michael Paterson writes, "Supervisors need to be people who have known . . . the vulnerability of trusting themselves into the loving hands of another as well as the power of being met with redemption rather than condemnation in admitting their weaknesses and mistakes."[18] Ultimately, vulnerability heightens ability to hear our supervisee.

SOME CROSS-CULTURAL SUPERVISION STORIES

At this point, I would like to change the "voice" to a more personal one as a means of illustrating some of the delights, challenges, and failings that others, too, may find in cross-cultural supervision. Most of the people I have supervised have come from non-Western backgrounds. They have been from a variety of cultures in the Pacific, from Korea, and from East Africa. They represent different denominations, different ministries, different genders and ages. It took me several years to appreciate how often we generalize "Pacific Islanders" without appreciating their own cultural differences. I have had the opportunity over the last thirty-five years to experience many cultural events, celebrations, and conversations with people whose heritage and traditions in the Pacific region are strong. I thought I understood a little, like the power of honor and shame, and the difference between shame and the Western more commonly spoken of "guilt."[19] I was on the lookout, as a supervi-

---

18. Leach and Paterson, *Pastoral Supervision*, 118.

19. Stephen Pattison writes of the feelings of self-censure and negative evaluation in Western culture that is often described as guilt, for which there are mechanisms such as confession and atonement. Shame however "is an acute, painful, inarticulate experience" for which there is no such remedy. "The shamed person is likely to feel a sense of personal collapse that implies

sor, for this. The theory might have been right, but it was head knowledge and the impact on practice was incomplete. This was brought home to me by a minister who apologized at the start of a session, saying he would need to go and check on some cakes that were in the oven. After a while he got up to look at the cakes. They needed a little longer, so we resumed as he talked about a ministry issue. He got up again and took the cakes out of the oven. I asked him about them, and he explained that he liked baking. He then said that he really enjoyed icing and decorating. These cakes were going to be part of a big celebration. I asked him if people knew about his talent. He replied that he could not tell people as it was really women's business. I wondered, aloud, what this was like for him, and he began to cry. What had started off as a casual interruption became a space of vulnerability in which he pondered how he would like to be understood and if it might be possible for him to model another way within his own circle—and what the costs might be. As a postlude, he began the next session by telling me, with a big smile, that he had proudly owned the decorated cakes as his. He was no longer ashamed of himself or of what others would think of him. He had been applauded.

Shame has many manifestations. Hewson describes shame as "a belief that there is something wrong with us."[20] In cross-cultural relationships, that can point to the differential we have noted where power lies with those whose background is white, who understand the language, its nuances, idioms, and complexities.[21] In supervision the differential enlarges the vulnerability and shame of the supervisee. On one occasion I was working with a woman whom I had supervised in different roles over some years. I had seen her grow in confidence although she still had some difficulty

---

the loss of self-esteem and self-efficacy." Pattison, *Shame: Theory, Therapy, Theology*, 43–44.

20. Hewson, "Passionate Supervision," 15.

21. Hawkins and Shohet emphasize that "Those who are 'white' need also to be aware of the power and privilege that this affords them." *Supervision*, 105, quoting Ryde, Judith. "Exploring White Racial Identity and Its Impact on Psychotherapy and the Psychotherapy Professions." PhD thesis, University of Bath, 2005.

with English and struggled with official church processes. She had often felt unseen and unable to be herself. In this session she talked about yet another incident that had again left her feeling disempowered. She seemed angry so I gently asked her what was going on at this moment. After a long pause she said she felt afraid. There was a silence when she struggled with tears. I again, gently probed what she was afraid of. She answered, "White people." I was stunned by her honesty, and, feeling helpless myself, affirmed her courage for naming this. It felt to me like a breakthrough, but the next morning there was an email from her telling me that she did not really mean what she had said. Clearly, it seemed to me, it was too hard to be honest, and she needed to rebuild her defenses. She was ashamed of what had happened and did not refer to this again. Her journey continues.

It is always a big step for any supervisee to speak about something that has been difficult rather than demonstrating that they are doing well enough. It takes time, trust, and courage. For some people who already feel culturally disadvantaged it can be particularly hard. This was made clear for me when supervising a priest from an Asian background who had been sent to minister within his own culture here in Australia. He needed to be seen to cope and, for some time, suggested that all was well. Gradually he admitted to feeling homesick and "down" and asked if I thought he should see a doctor. Eventually he was diagnosed with depression and put on medication. At this low point he began to use our sessions to describe his feelings and speak about the things he was doing to try and cope. He spoke of his shame. It was profoundly moving.

Vulnerability, awkwardness, and powerlessness were illustrated again in a session with a minister from an Asian background in her first congregation. There are gaps in her command of English which make life difficult for her. She talked of the difficulties she experienced working with the lay leadership in her congregation. She had previously spoken about feeling bullied. As the session came toward a close, she said that what was happening was racism. It was a statement of truth for her that was hard to hear. There was a transference of powerlessness in the moment. It also became a key, because having used the word *racism* once, she felt able to use it again in other sessions which led on to her describing the anger she felt. It was "like a volcano." The volcano has become a metaphor not just for anger but for power within.

Another aspect of power imbalance, perceived hierarchy, and vulnerability emerges when the supervisee wants to use it primarily as an opportunity to ask for advice. A dilemma may be presented to me as the one with knowledge, the wisdom. It is often hard to tease this out and explore beyond the facts. A pattern may well be a culturally derived view of the "elder," or person with authority, who is held in respect while the younger person listens. In addition, it may be a strange and awkward expectation for the supervisee to reflect as an individual with another individual. It potentially opens them up to personal shame of failure. It may not be the natural way for them to reflect on issues. In many Pacific cultures, the way of sharing is communal, through story.[22] Men gather around a bowl of kava and sit and listen to one another, knowing there is room for understanding. For women that happens more informally, yet intentionally, around the kitchen bench preparing the food. Supervision with one individual may not be the most suitable approach.

In Western culture, as in supervision, the verbal exploration of feelings is often seen as the way to deeper reflection, a healthy path to self-understanding. There are vulnerabilities for those for whom English is a second language. Apart from the cultural reticence mentioned above, finding words to express feelings may be difficult. The language of the heart is less accessible. This became evident in a session with a young woman who became silent when I asked her about something she had said. She did want to respond but simply could not find the right words. It felt awkward. I asked her if she could think of it in her own language. After a pause she nodded and then used her phone and Google Translate to tell me. She had felt unsure of herself. A lot was being asked of her.

22. See Tu'iono, "Seeking to Create 'Vā' Spaces."

In contrast, for some formed by an oral tradition, speaking their way through an issue may place the supervisor in a different place. This was the case when a man I had worked with for a long time told me at the beginning of the session that he had something he wanted to talk about. In the end, he spoke for almost the whole hour. There were pauses as he processed internally what he was saying. I said nothing. His body language indicated that he had not finished what he wanted to express. At the end I briefly acknowledged him, and he affirmed the place he had reached in his exploration. He had heard himself speak outside his culture and had understood what he was feeling in the broader context. I continue to learn about remaining silent.

CONCLUSION

Writing of these examples is not about examining how I worked as a supervisor, but rather to illustrate some of the aspects of vulnerability that I have discovered in myself and for my supervisees. The realization that we all come into the supervision space formed from both our individual and cultural backgrounds, recognizing that none of us is neutral, is a gift if we allow ourselves to own it and can be vulnerable enough to explore it. That very vulnerability can be the basis for rich and empathetic relationship. We create a safe and respectful supervision space where insights into culture emerge and can be explored in an Australian context. It is always a special privilege to be entrusted with things that lie close to someone's heart. Shared, unspoken awareness of vulnerability becomes opportunity when held with care and respect.

BIBLIOGRAPHY

DeYmaz, Mark. *Building a Healthy Multi-Ethnic Church*. Hoboken, NJ: Wiley, 2007.
DiAngelo, Robin. *White Fragility: Why It's So Hard for White People to Talk About Racism*. London: Penguin, 2018. Fopp, Rodney. *Enhancing Understanding: Advancing Dialogue*. Adelaide, Australia: ATF, 2008.

Hawkins, Peter. Foreword to *Passionate Supervision*, edited by Robin Shohet, 9–12. London: Jessica Kingsley, 2008.

Hawkins, Peter and Robin Shohet. *Supervision in the Helping Professions*. 3rd ed. Maidenhead, UK: Open University, 2006.

Hewson, Julie. "Passionate Supervision: A Wider Landscape." In *Passionate Supervision*, edited by Robin Shohet, 33–48. London: Jessica Kingsley, 2008.

Johnson, Lydia F. *Drinking From the Same Well: Cross-Cultural Concerns in Pastoral Care and Counseling*. Eugene, OR: Wipf and Stock, 2011.

Leach, Jane, and Michael Paterson. *Pastoral Supervision: A Handbook*. 2nd ed. London: SCM, 2015.

Pattison, Stephen. *Shame: Theory, Therapy, Theology*. Cambridge: Cambridge University Press, 2000.

Pearson, Clive. "Imagining a Reformed Practical Theology and Ethics." In *Imagining a Way: Exploring Reformed Practical Theology and Ethics*, edited by Clive Pearson, 3–35. Louisville: Westminster John Knox, 2017.

Shohet, Robin. "Fear and Love In and Beyond Supervision." In *Passionate Supervision*, edited by Robin Shohet, 187–208. London: Jessica Kingsley, 2008.

Tu'iono, Kamaloni. "Seeking to Create 'Vā' Spaces as a Means of Fostering a Communal Model of Supervision in a Cross-Cultural Setting." PhD thesis, Charles Sturt University, 2021.

Notes on the Contributors

Rev. Dr. Sang Taek Lee OAM is the Principal and CEO of Iona Trinity College of Higher Education, a CPE supervisor, a member of the Advisory Committee of the Mental Health CPE Centre, and a minister of the Uniting Church in Australia. Sang Taek received his PhD degree from the University of Sydney. He is the author of a number of books, including *Religion and Social Formation in Korea: Minjung and Millennial Hope* (Mouton de Gruyter, Berlin/New York). He is the co-editor of *You Visited Me: Encouraging Spiritual Practice in a Secular World* (2021).

Rev. Alan Galt OAM, Centre Director and CPE Education Consultant, has been a Uniting Church Minister since 1966, and is a Fellow of the NSW College of CPE. He studied Psychology and Anthropology at the University of Sydney, and Theology at the Methodist Theological College and Melbourne College of Divinity. A Mental Health Chaplain for 35 years, and a CPE supervisor for 40 years, he has been Secretary of the NSW Council (now College) for CPE, Convenor of its Accreditation sub-committee, and Academic Dean. He is the co-editor of *You Visited Me: Encouraging Spiritual Practice in a Secular World* (2021).

Dr. Nicola Le Couteur works as a Clinical Pastoral Supervisor for the Mental Health CPE Centre in NSW, Australia, and in private practice. Her passion is supporting people to follow their calling into spiritual care practice, as well as pursuing her own practice of spiritual care in psychiatric settings. Nicola loves wilderness hiking, embracing the challenges of navigation, ever-changing territory and camaraderie in equal measure!

Debra Kelly has co-supervised at both St Vincent's Hospital and the Mental Health CPE Centres. She has a BD from London and an MA in Buddhism from Sydney. Having taught Secondary Religious Education, she then discovered the world of chaplaincy and was Buddhist Chaplain at the University of Technology. Since 2019, she has been in the Pastoral Care Team at St Vincent's Private Hospital. A Zen student, Debra continues to explore the integration of Buddhist teachings with holistic care and supervision.

Rev. Dr. Peter Powell is a Uniting Church in Australia minister, a Teacher with the Sydney College of Divinity, a Registered Psychologist, a Clinical Member of the Australian and New Zealand Association for the Treatment of Sexual Abusers, and a Clinical Member of the NSW Child Sex Offender Counsellors Accreditation Scheme. Peter is a Provisional Education Consultant with the NSW College of Clinical Pastoral Education. He graduated from the Garrett-Evangelical Theological Seminary, Illinois (Doctoral degree in Pastoral Counselling and Psychotherapy). Peter is Past President of the NSW College of Clinical Pastoral Education.

Associate Professor Salih Yucel received a Bachelor of Islamic Theology from the University of Ankara, and a Master of Theology from the University of Sydney. His doctoral research, conducted at Boston University, examined the effects of prayer on Muslim patients' well-being. He teaches at the Centre for Islamic Studies and Civilisation at Charles Sturt University, and is a Provisional Clinical Pastoral Educator at the Australia and New Zealand Association for Clinical Pastoral Education. Salih has authored four books and a number of articles.

Krsnangi Mulder is a Trauma Informed Karuna Care Chaplain, Provisional Pastoral Supervisor, and member of the Mental Health CPE Centre and NSW College of CPE, engaged in aged care and mental health ministries. A retired Hare Krsna Temple Priest, she has also been a women's (Vaisnavi) sanga and community radio program co-ordinator, teacher of Vedic Scripture classes in NSW schools, and member of the Gaudiya Vaisnava faith community. She holds a Diploma of Holistic Counselling and Life Care, and is involved in community education, health, and wellness programs, including those supporting culturally and linguistically diverse communities.

Barbara Hall is a Pastoral Supervisor in private practice, Pastoral Educator with NSW College of Clinical Pastoral Education, currently holding the position of College President, and an Associate Teacher with Sydney College of Divinity. Barbara lives in Goulburn NSW with her husband, where they raised four children and are now blessed with seven grandchildren. With 30 years' experience as a pastoral care practitioner in acute, palliative, rehabilitation and psychiatric hospital settings, Barbara held the position of Coordinator, Chaplaincy & Pastoral Care for 17 of those years.

Rosemarie Say OAM is an Associate Teacher with the Sydney College of Divinity, CPE Educator and full-time Mental Health Chaplain. After winning the Gold Medal for Psychiatric Nursing, she graduated in 2010 with an MA (Pastoral Supervision). Following over 20 years of volunteer work, she was awarded a Medal of the Order of Australia (OAM) in 2015 "For service to community health, particularly mental health services".

Susanne Schmidt is a CPE Educator with the NSW College of CPE (Australia). She is the National Pastoral Care Educator for Calvary Australia. Her interests in spiritual care include good clinical documentation, emerging expressions of spirituality, and psychedelics and spiritual care. Other interests include reading (she aims to break her current record of 200 books in a year!) and travel; the current big trip is the Silk Road, and the next one is a return trip to a much visited place, Hawaii, for a milestone birthday.

Rev. Mary Pearson is a retired Uniting Church minister. Previously, in Scotland, she was a member of The Iona Community, a teacher of the deaf, trained in counselling, and worked for the Save the Children Fund before emigrating to New Zealand and then Australia. She trained as a pastoral supervisor with Transforming Practices and is now a supervisor trainer with Transforming Practices and the Australasian Association of Supervision. She has particular interest in cross-cultural supervision and working with difference.

www.ingramcontent.com/pod-product-compliance
Lightning Source LLC
Chambersburg PA
CBHW051103160426
43193CB00010B/1297